"This is a unique and effective .... w understanding the structure of films they are familiar with. It covers
the important terrain of character and story action and interaction without being a rule book."

—Academy Award-winning screenwriter ALVIN SARGENT,
Ordinary People, Paper Moon

"Dr. Li .... ore. She
takes t .... hers and
explair .... ovides a
magic .... grab this
book a ....

.... *rom The*
.... *reenplay*

"At last .... s. Richly
detaile .... ution to
the art ....

.... *r's Bible*

"An in .... es, and
details .... hwriting
which .... er stand
out in t ....

—K .... *g Game*

"Linda .... lyzes in
depth a .... sive insights ir .... aluable
to the v .... heartily
recomm .... a good
script and wants to make it a winner."

—screenwriter D. C. FONTANA, *Star Trek, Dallas*

ADVANCED
SCREENWRITING

Other books by Linda Seger

Screenwriting Books

Making a Good Script Great
Creating Unforgettable Characters
The Art of Adaptation: Turning Fact and Fiction into Film
From Script to Screen: The Collaborative Art of Filmmaking
*When Women Call the Shots: The Developing Power and
Influence of Women in Television and Film*
Making a Good Writer Great

Non-Fiction Books

Web-Thinking: Connecting, not Competing for Success

ADVANCED SCREENWRITING

Raising your Script to the Academy Award Level

DR. LINDA SEGER

SILMAN-JAMES PRESS ■ LOS ANGELES

First Edition
10 9 8 7 6 5 4 3 2 1

Library of Congress Cataloging-in-Publication Data

Seger, Linda
Advanced Screenwriting: Raising Your Script to the Academy Award
Level / by Linda Seger.
p.   cm.

ISBN: 1-879505-73-8

Cover design by Heidi Frieder

Printed and bound in the United States of America

Silman-James Press
1181 Angelo Drive
Beverly Hills, CA 90210

To my dear friends, who are also dedicated screenwriting teachers and script consultants:

Carolyn Miller
Kathie Fong Yoneda
Rachel Ballon
Pamela Jaye Smith
Devorah Cutler-Rubinstein
Karen Jacobs
Mara Purl

Acknowledgments

With many thanks to my publishers—Gwen Feldman and Jim Fox—for their support of my work and for Jim's excellent editing.

To Dr. Leonard Felder, for the title.

To my brilliant assistant, Robin Rindner, for her knowledge and support, day and night, and to my brilliant researcher, Sue Terry, who knows where to find everything and never lets me down.

Thank you to my amazing readers, whose feedback, notes, ideas, additional examples, knowledge about the field of screenwriting, and constant support is a true dialogue and collaboration between us: Beth Brickell, Heidi Boyden, Devorah Cutler-Rubinstein, Karen Jacobs, Pamela Jaye Smith, Sandi Steinberg, and Susie Stroh.

And always, thank you to my dear husband, Peter Hazen Le Var.

Acknowledgments for quoted materials are noted on the following page.

The author gratefully acknowledges and thanks the following for permission to quote from their work:

to Writers Lawrence Kasdan and Frank Galati for permission to quote from *The Accidental Tourist*, from the book by Anne Tyler, a Warner Bros. production.

Dreamworks for permission to quote from *American Beauty*, screenplay by Allan Ball.

Universal Studios for permission to quote from *Babe*, screenplay by George Miller and Chris Noonan.

Universal Studios and Akiva Goldsman for permission to quote from *A Beautiful Mind*, screenplay by Akiva Goldsman, based on the book *A Beautiful Mind* by Sylvia Nasar.

Universal Studios for permission to quote from *Born on the Fourth of July*, screenplay by Ron Kovic and Oliver Stone, based on the book by Ron Kovic.

MGM Studios for permission to quote from *Bull Durham*, screenplay by Ron Shelton.

to Screenwriter Menno Meyjes and agent Tim Osborne for permission to quote from *The Color Purple*, based on the book *The Color Purple* by Alice Walker, a Warner Bros. picture.

Screenwriter Christopher Hampton for permission to quote from *Dangerous Liaisons*, a Warner Bros. production.

Screenwriter Gary Ross for permission to quote from *Dave*, a Warner Brothers Studios release.

Screenwriter Tom Schulman for permission to quote from *Dead Poets Society*, a Silver Screen Partners IV, Touchstone Pictures Production.

Screenwriters Joel and Ethan Coen for permission to quote from *Fargo*, Gramercy Pictures, PolyGram Filmed Entertainment, Working Title Films Production.

Screenwriter Aaron Sorkin for permission to quote from *A Few Good Men*, a Columbia/Tristar production.

The Rod Hall Agency, Ltd., and screenwriter Simon Beaufoy for permission to quote from *The Full Monty*, a Channel Four Films and Redwave Productions film.

Screenwriter Bruce Joel Rubin for permission to quote from *Ghost*, a Paramount Studios picture.

Screenwriter Frank Darabont for permission to quote from his script for *The Green Mile*, based on the book by Stephen King, a Castle Rock Entertainment, Darkwoods Productions, and Warner Bros. film.

Newmarket Films for permission to quote from *Memento*, screenplay by Christopher Nolan.

to MGM Studios for permission to quote from *Moonstruck*, screenplay by John Patrick Shanley.

to Screenwriter Shane Connaughton for permission to quote from *My Left Foot*, a Granada Studios production.

to Agent Simon Trewin and screenwriter Richard Curtis for permission to quote from *Notting Hill*, a Bookshop Productions, Notting Hill Pictures, PolyGram Filmed Entertainment, and Working Title Films production.

Universal Studios for permission to quote from *On Golden Pond*, screenplay by Ernest Thompson.

Screenwriters Scott Alexander and Larry Karaszewski for permission to quote from *The People vs. Larry Flynt*, a Columbia Pictures production.

to MGM Studios and Barry Morrow for permission to quote from *Rain Man*, screenplay by Barry Morrow and Ron Bass.

to Universal Studios for permission to quote from *Schindler's List*, screenplay by Steve Zaillian, from the book *Schindler's List* by Thomas Keneally.

to Screenwriter, Mike Leigh, for permission to quote from *Secrets & Lies*, a Channel Four Films, CiBy 2000, Thin Man Films production.

to Screenwriter Emma Thompson for permission to quote from *Sense and Sensibility*, a Columbia Pictures production.

to Screenwriter Scott Hicks for permission to quote from *Shine*, a Australian Film Finance Corporation, Film Victoria, Momentum Films production.

to MGM Studios for permission to quote from *Silence of the Lambs*, screenplay by Ted Tally, based on the book *Silence of the Lambs* by Thomas Harris.

to Writers Larry Gelbart, Murray Schisgal, and actor Dustin Hoffman for permission to quote from *Tootsie*, story by Don McGuire and Larry Gelbart, screenplay by Larry Gelbart and Murray Schisgal, a Columbia/Tri-Star picture.

to Screenwriter Stephan Gaghan for permission to quote from *Traffic*, a Bedford Falls Productions, Compulsion Inc., Initial Entertainment Group, Splendid Medien, USA Films production.

to Screenwriters Earl Wallace and Pamela Wallace for permission to quote from *Witness*, story by William Kelley, Earl Wallace, Pamela Wallace, screenplay by William Kelley and Earl Wallace, a Paramount Picture.

to Screenwriter Kevin Wade for permission to quote from *Working Girl*, a 20th Century Fox production.

Contents

Introduction

By the year 2000, almost 200 books about basic screenwriting were on the market. These books—along with thousands of screenwriting seminars and the script consultants and story analysts who have analyzed innumerable scripts—have helped advance the craft of writing. In my twenty years consulting on more than 2,000 scripts and teaching screenwriting in more than twenty countries, I have been impressed with writers' commitment to learning the complex art and craft of screenwriting.

While applauding the increased competence in scriptwriting, I want more: I want to see more innovation in the art of storytelling. I'd like to see new subject matter and new forms to express new types of stories. I want to see more producers and executives recognize a great script when they see one, and recognize the difference between something merely different and something exceptional. I want to see great art and great craft. I want to see an increased respect for bold, courageous, and masterful screenwriting.

This book is about details. It's about all the intricate, complex script elements that make it possible for films like *Magnolia* and *The Hours* to become great films when their very structures invite failure. It's about creating a script that moves well, with a story that is focused and original and leaps off the page. It's about creating a script that gives a great actor something to work with. It's about creating a script that integrates its various elements of story, character, theme, and style into a cohesive whole. Beyond that, it's about creating stories that touch and intrigue an audience and perhaps transform lives in the process.

I see this book as more than just an analysis of screen-writing techniques and why they work. I see it as a way to encourage you to think differently about your approaches to your work. Throughout the book I ask questions about the films I discuss: Did it work for you? Do you think this technique could have worked better with a slightly different approach?

Sometimes I might admire a technique in a film but believe it could have been better executed. Sometimes, I might admire a part of a film that you feel could have been rendered with more sophistication. I may critique some Academy Award-winning films that you consider perfect. However, regardless of my opinion, I always ask of every film, What can we learn from this film that can advance the art of scriptwriting?

Since this is a book about the future of screenwriting, I chose to limit my examples. Most of the films I'll discuss are Academy Award winners or nominees from 1980 to the present. Although I admire many of the classics, most of them are not good models for the future. Occasionally I will go beyond Academy Award nominees to a few that never got the attention of the Academy, but which I personally admire. Very occasionally I will mention a familiar classic that best exemplifies an idea.

If you are reading this book, you have most likely read some basic scriptwriting books, taken some seminars, and written some scripts. Some of you may have won awards for your work. I hope all of you have a desire to go further with your art—to learn new techniques, to consider new possibilities, to figure out how to make something new and different work.

While each of my earlier books can stand alone, this one builds on the knowledge offered in my basic screenwriting books and is meant to be a sequel. It builds particularly on the techniques discussed in *Making a Good Script Great, Creating Unforgettable Characters,* and *Making a Good Writer Great.* Although I try not to repeat material from these books, there are times when some of the previous material is mentioned in order to build further on it.

I hope this book will stretch you as it has stretched me. I hope that it encourages you to find new subject matter and new forms to express your ideas. I hope it encourages you to learn new skills and to continually be original. Most of all, I hope it increases your passion for one of the youngest art forms—the art of film.

1

A Realistic Tale
Well Told

Many writers begin to write because of a need to express themselves. They have attitudes, values, and insights they want to convey. They feel the nudge and push of their stories. They want to give life to their characters.

For most writers, the next step is learning the craft of writing—learning how to construct a script and how to structure it to best express what they want to say. They learn three-act structure and how to set up, develop, and pay off a story. They use twists and turns to enrich the story. They become visual thinkers, using images to express their ideas. They gain proficiency in paying attention to details—the small quirks and flaws that bring characters to life.

As most writers develop further, they learn how every choice affects every other choice. They see the relationships of their character arcs and the expression of their ideas. They see the relationships of their images to the genre they're working in.

Good writers are continually in training to be great writers. They're alert. Aware. They notice details. They seek out experiences and reflect on them. They have a point of view. They tell us what matters to them and what's it all about. They express meaning. They are interpreters of the world. A great writer is part problem-solver, part strategist, part thinker, and part truth-teller.

Great writers create from the fabric of their lives. They're not afraid to experience the ups and downs of life, which give them something to create from. Great writers imagine. They visualize. They present their fictional world in a unique way and help us see life from a fresh perspective. Great writers have a voice—and they're not afraid to let it be heard.

Great writers go one step further than good writers. They think of the audience. They don't just think of how they can get millions of people to come to their film, but how to clearly communicate their ideas in ways that will excite, enthrall, and engage an audience. They know what to hide and what to reveal and when to reveal it. They develop a sense of how the audience feels at various points in their stories. At what moment do they expect the audience to fall in love with the lead character? At what moment might they lose the audience? How sympathetic does a character have to be in order to keep the audience connected? How will the audience identify with the story, even though it might be a period piece or science fiction or just plain quirky? How can they layer their films so that the audience wants to see them again and again, finding new wonders in each viewing?

Great writers are courageous and bold. They're willing to experiment with new subject matter, new ideas, new structures. They're willing to dream, to explore, to use their imagination. And they're willing to rise to the challenge of figuring out how to make their experiments work.

Think about the originality of such past Academy Award winning writers as Steven Zaillian (*Schindler's List*), Akiva Goldsman (*A Beautiful Mind*), the Coen brothers (*Fargo*), Christopher McQuarrie (*The Usual Suspects*), Marc Norman and Tom Stoppard (*Shakespeare in Love*), Jane Campion (*The Piano*), and Neil Jordan (*The Crying Game*). Each of these writers went out on a limb. Each one did something original and made it work. Each created great drama.

What is great drama? Here's my criteria:

- Passion. A character's passion for justice. A burning desire to right a wrong. A yearning to love madly, truly, deeply.

- Characters we care about in a story worth caring about.
- Characters making decisions and willing to face the consequences of those decisions. Something that must be done, and characters willing to do it, no matter what the cost.
- High stakes. A seemingly insurmountable conflict. A resistance to be confronted. An obstacle to be overcome.
- Momentum. Anticipation. Something is ready to happen. Something *is* happening.

Think about how this criteria applies to recent Academy Award winners such as *American Beauty, A Beautiful Mind, Silence of the Lambs, Shakespeare in Love,* and *Chicago.*

We're not born with an ability to create great drama, although some people seem to be natural storytellers. The ability to write well and create great drama can be learned and developed. As writers learn more about the art of dramatic writing, they begin to broaden and deepen their work, creating new forms, finding new stories to tell and new ways of telling them, creating memorable scripts that continue to expand the possibilities of film.

THE LINEAR STRUCTURE IN DRAMA

Drama shows and helps clarify the meaning—or the lack of it—in our lives. And drama needs a structure to convey its meaning.

Since the early 1990s, we have seen much experimentation with story structure as writers try to find new patterns that express a broad understanding of our lives—to encompass the complexity, dualities, and multiple realities of our lives. They've looked for ways to move beyond traditional linear structure, to find cinematic structures that express the many non-linear patterns we perceive in our lives. What are these patterns? How do they work? Where do they fail? What are the problems writers encounter when they move beyond traditional structures? How are they solved?

Western culture has some prevailing ideas about the definition of a story. A story is a series of events, with a beginning, a middle, and an end. It has a main character who tries to achieve a goal, confronting obstacles along the way. It's about development, processes, and journeys.

Most dramatic stories are linear because they're based on our primary understanding of time. We see the passage of time in our lives as an accumulation of connected experiences that we hope will add up to something meaningful. All Western cultures and most Eastern cultures understand the progression of time as a linear stream of events. This understanding of time is not the only one there is, but it's the most prevalent one, and it's the basis of most drama.

The first stories may have been dramas about a lion hunt that were re-enacted around the campfire. This story easily falls into a three-act structure: the preparation, the hunt, the climactic event when the lion is killed, and the resolution of the celebration feast afterward. It contains many elements we associate with drama: conflict, action, tension, and momentum.

Like our lion-hunting ancestors, we tell our stories as linear events. We say, "And then this happened, and then he said that, and then I did this."

Or we say, "I met him and we started to date and for a while everything was all right and then there was all sorts of trouble, but at the end we got married and everything is now going very well and guess what, I'm pregnant."

Or: "He decided to climb Everest and he trained for about a year, but when he got to the mountain he found the climb much more difficult than he expected it to be and at one point he almost died, but at the end he made it and we're really glad he's home now."

Or: "She got cancer, which was such a shock to all of us, and she went through treatment, but it didn't work, and her doctors finally tried a new experimental therapy that was just horrendous. Oh, the trouble she went through, but then it all began to come together and she's been doing just fine for the last two years."

These linear structures have hundreds of variations: stories about the person who won the contest or defeated the villain or founded the new colony or protected the family.

The ancient Greeks, the ancient Romans, the sixteenth century Commedia dell'Arte players, dramatists Christopher Marlowe and William Shakespeare, and most writers up to the present have expressed their dramatic stories as linear structures.

Linear stories generally are told as a progression through three acts. The story starts with a setup, which presents a story's context and provides an event that begins the story. The setup also introduces us to a story's major characters. In Act Two, a story's conflicts and theme and character relationships develop, relying on action to propel the story forward. Act Three pays off the actions of Act Two with a climax. If Act Two involves an investigation, then the pay-off shows the results of the investigation. If the story is about an illness and a character who does whatever is necessary to cure it, in the third act, the character either gets sicker and dies or gets well. If the story's a romance, Act Two develops the love story, and we see the result of that development in Act Three. You can't get to Act Three without going through Act Two, although many writers would like to.

Although some writers think of these ideas as following a formula, I don't believe that drama has rules. It has concepts and principles about how best to tell a story. Drama, like all art, has form. It's up to a writer to find the best form for a particular story.

Structure is not meant to be a limit, but a shape to help focus a story so an audience can understand what's going on and not get lost or disoriented. Structure helps a writer express a particular interpretation of events, clarify what a story is about, and keeps that story on a clear track. Art is not about confusion, fooling the audience, throwing everything in with the kitchen sink, and creating chaos.

STORYTELLING PATTERNS

Most stories (and all linear ones) are based on the belief that events are the result of cause and effect. We build on the information, actions, and learning that have gone before.

The linear storytelling structure usually contains certain presumptions: Most linear films are goal-oriented, built on the presumption that achieving a goal defines a person's value. Determination, will, courage, and action are considered exemplary qualities. Characters try, and try some more. They confront obstacles. Embedded in linear storytelling is the idea that the ending is the result of everything that has gone before, and that the end usually justifies the means. Linear storytelling implies that life normally moves toward desired improvement and inevitable resolution and that good should win over evil. It implies that "every day in every way we're getting better and better."

But a linear progression of events is not the only way to view our lives. In certain non-Western cultures, the telling of stories is not linear. Sometimes these cultures create films that strike most Western viewers as being "outside" the commonly accepted notions of time. Some cultures, such as the Maoris as well as some Eastern cultures and Native American cultures, tend to see time as primarily the individual present moment. They don't choose to look at the world as a series of cause-and-effect processes. Traditional Balinese culture doesn't view life as a process of changes, but as a steady state. To show a story as a progression would imply the Western idea that our world is changing.

Many of us raised in a Western culture also perceive non-linear patterns in our lives that can be rendered into stories. Our lives often include long passages of relative inactivity: internal quests for meaning, dreams and reflections, working through depressions, and contemplating the importance of money, success, and happiness.

Life also can be about individual moments that may not fit well into a traditional story template, and yet, they define us and change us: the time you won an award, the time you first met the blond-haired boy in second grade and thought you would die with love.

Because of the many differences in how we see our lives, drama has the potential to interpret life and communicate via many different patterns. New forms and new structures can lead us to new understandings of our own lives as well as the lives of those from other cultures.

THE JOURNEY STORY

Since most people view drama as progression and development, most of our dramas are journey stories, which usually involve an external journey. The characters in these dramas don't necessarily have to go somewhere, but the development of a particular situation takes the characters through certain events that move the story forward and may transform the characters in the process. These events provide the energy, the motor of the story, keeping it moving forward. Each event and action has consequences that create the need for more actions. These, in turn, create reactions. And more action. And more reaction. There is cause and effect.

Events don't need to be highly dramatic to provide a story with a motor. A character who is dying (*Magnolia, One True Thing, Philadelphia*) or about to die (*Saving Private Ryan, The Green Mile*) raises basic human issues that force development and conflict.

A search for love (*Sense and Sensibility, When Harry Met Sally, Sleepless in Seattle, Shakespeare in Love, Il Postino, Babe*) provides enough energy for a story to progress. Events can be big or small, but the journey story builds on these events and shapes these events to help us understand the development of our own lives.

THE DESCRIPTIVE STORY

In some rare American films, and in a number of international films, the story does not focus on a progression of events, but describes a situation. It tells us, "This is the way it is." A film shows a character caught in a context. Descriptive films can show a slice of life, sometimes highlighting the static nature and the repetition of our lives. In these films, the characters are often the victims of events, rather than the movers of events. The movers are often off-screen, and sometimes have little interaction with the characters who are caught by their decisions.

One of the best examples of this type of film is *Au Revoir Les Enfants*, the French film nominated for Best Picture Academy Award in 1988. The story is about as small as one could have. A boy is sent away to school during Germany's occupation of France in World War II. There, he develops a friendship with a Jewish boy who is hidden at the school. Finally, the Jewish boy is discovered and taken away by the Germans.

The motor for the story is off-screen. It comes from the Germans. We rarely see them and have no idea who might have betrayed the boy, or whether he really was betrayed. How the boy's Jewishness affected others is never explored. We see suspicious schoolmates who try to discover if he is or isn't Jewish. But there's little focus on the boys finding any new understanding as a result of having a Jew in their midst or as a result of his betrayal. There's no focus on the dynamic between the Germans and the school, or the potential danger. The film shows the situation. This is how it was. Jewish boys were sometimes hidden in schools, and sometimes they were discovered.

I have trouble with a film such as *Au Revoir Les Enfants*, because the rich dramatic conflict embedded in the context of its story isn't explored. It's as if the filmmaker shied away from the drama in order to create intriguing images and characters. Although sometimes such films are nominated for Academy Awards for their rich imagery and emotional content, most of the time they die quickly at the box office because there is little drama to grab audiences. American cinema has produced few descriptive films, and even in European films such films are rare. Although many non-American films will be slower-paced and often more character-driven than American films, most of their storylines have some momentum and move forward toward a goal and a climax. Such films include *Kolya, The Wedding Banquet, Antonia's Line, Crouching Tiger, Hidden Dragon, Life Is Beautiful,* and *Indochine.*

A short list of American descriptive films could include *My Dinner with Andre, Swimming to Cambodia,* and *Terms of Endearment.* The most successful of these films was the Academy Award-winning *Terms of Endearment.* The film is somewhat episodic, covering events in the relationship of a mother and daughter. It doesen't provide a strong goal or character intention. It describes and follows a relationship that moves through ups and downs, crises, and challenges. The film finds its momentum through the conflicts and subplots that revolve around the relationships of mother-daughter, daughter-husband, and the mother's developing relationship with the astronaut who lives next door. It contains more momentum and conflict than most descriptive films, but it lacks the strong narrative line that is found in most journey films.

In any descriptive film, a writer asks some of the same questions that would be posed for any more traditional story: Where is the engine that moves the story? Where is the conflict? Where is the energy coming from?

A descriptive film usually demands more patience from the audience since it does not move toward a single specific goal. It is often reactive, rather than pro-active, and may even seem static. Although most of us were probably very involved with the characters in *Terms of Endearment,* in many other descriptive films we may feel as if we're sitting way back—distant from the events in a film. We may not care about the characters as much because a story's unclear about exactly who and what we're rooting for.

Descriptive films are usually slower-paced than journey films. Often they seem to have little forward action or movement. Therefore, the success of such a film depends on whether the audience identifies with its characters and situations, and is concerned for them. At its best, it gives us insight into some aspect of the human condition. At its worst, it's like watching paint dry.

When done well, a descriptive film can give full play to other elements of drama: style, depth, and originality of character, charming scenes, and unforgettable images. And in most descriptive films, you find some semblance of a linear progression toward a climax, but rarely with a strong structure. You might find a catalyst—an event that starts the story. You might find an occasional turning point—an event that turns the direction of the story as it moves from act to act. But turning points are often missing and the climax might be diffused rather than forceful. The focus in such films is often on individual scenes or the texture or mood of the experience, rather than on the logical sequencing of events.

If you choose to do a descriptive film, try to give it some forward movement and some semblance of a three-act structure. Look for any implied conflict that may be part of a story's context. Rather than dissipating it, explore it.

REPETITIVE STRUCTURES

In the last twenty years, we've seen a number of new structures that experiment with the traditional linear structure. Some of these structures express the non-linear patterns in our lives. Some of these patterns are repetitive. We become like a broken record, replaying the same negative situations in our lives over and over. We date the same kind of abusive people, we get into the same dead-end jobs, we fight an ongoing struggle with our vices and our resolutions to improve ourselves—perhaps over-eating followed by the commitment to diet; gambling, struggling with money, and gambling some more;

perhaps trying to stop drinking, drinking, and trying to stop again. In the broken-record structure, we never get beyond the problems that plague us. We just don't seem to get it, and the process circles around and round, like a record that can never finish its song. We're stuck. We can't seem to move. Nothing new happens.

The broken-record structure is found in *Groundhog Day*. The film doesn't have a nice, neat development, but utilizes the pattern of repetition. Generally, repetition is not dramatic because it simply shows us what we've seen before. It can get boring. It usually isn't suited to drama, which is intrinsically about development and about moving forward. And yet, repetitive life patterns are very real. We all experience them. We all can relate to them.

Why was *Groundhog Day* so successful, even though its structure was built on the pattern of repetition? *Groundhog Day* uses a number of elements from traditional structure. It tells a story about a man who repeats Groundhog Day over and over again, until he finally understands what he's supposed to learn and is able to move on with his life.

Groundhog Day has a clear beginning, middle, and end, but the middle repeats itself seven times, creating a beginning, middle, middle, middle, middle, middle, middle, middle, and end. Phil starts his repetitive day at the story's first turning point and ends it at the second turning point. However, while exploring repetition in the second act, the story also develops. Each time the lesson repeats, something is added, so we feel that we are still moving forward, albeit via baby steps for much of the second act. A compelling reason is needed to move beyond repetition. In this case, the compelling reason is Rita.

If you use a repetitive structure, make sure there's some forward movement and some variety so that the audience doesn't simply see the same scene again and again. Otherwise, audiences can feel stuck, bored, and frustrated.

When using a repetitive structure, part of a writer's job is to figure out at what point the audience gets the point that is conveyed through repetition. In early drafts of *Field of Dreams*, several scenes showed Ray Kinsella's resistance to building a baseball field in the middle of Iowa. The screenwriter, Phil Alden Robinson, struggled with the number of repetitions he would need before the audience could suspend their disbelief about Ray's actions. He found, when testing the film, that he had included one too many, so a scene was cut.

In *Breaking the Waves*, when Bess McNeill says goodbye to her husband as he returns to the oil rig, she kisses him, moves away, runs to him, kisses him, moves away, runs to him, kisses him, moves away. You might want to re-watch this film to see when you understood the point of the scene, and whether the film repeated what you already understood.

Another film that uses a similar repetitive pattern is the German film *Run Lola Run*. Instead of using a beginning, middle, end, it plays out its story three times with different endings. It uses the structure of beginning, middle, end, beginning, middle, and end, beginning, middle, end, with each section divided by a bridge, where the lovers talk. It borrowed its structure from interactive games that use repetition to explore an idea about which choices yield the best results. *Run Lola Run* explored a relationship to see which choice best served that relationship.

PARALLEL STRUCTURES

Parallel journeys

Most films have a major plotline (or "A"story) with subplots that relate to that main plotline, pushing at it and intersecting it. However, some films work with parallel storylines rather than intersecting storylines.

In real life, stories go on all around us all the time. Sometimes they intersect our lives. Sometimes they parallel our lives. While you're developing your writing career, a producer in Beverly Hills and a director from Canada are also developing their respective careers. Each of these three lives has its own direction. Each continues with little or no regard for the others. But, at some point, perhaps, the three will intersect and you'll get your movie made.

Parallel structures are not subplots. A subplot serves and supports the main storyline. It dimensionalizes and intersects the main story. In parallel journey structures, each storyline has equal weight. Although, eventually, they connect in most films, each has its own structure and its own movement.

We see examples of parallel journeys in many traditional films in which one character is introduced first and starts her story, and then another character is introduced and starts his story. In most cases, these parallel journeys will intersect at either the end of the setup or at the first turning point. However, there are exceptions. *Sleepless in Seattle* uses the parallel-journey structure until its very end, when the two lovers meet. *Do the Right Thing* shows the parallel journeys of all its characters living through a hot day, only occasionally meeting each other, until they all intersect in the film's violent climactic scenes. In *Secrets & Lies*, Cynthia's life and Hortense's life parallel each other until they intersect at the film's midpoint. In *Crouching Tiger, Hidden Dragon*, the two women's stories sometimes parallel each other and sometimes intersect. *The Hours* shows three parallel journeys from three different time periods. The film implies a relationship between these three stories, and two of the storylines intersect in Act Three.

Sliding Doors begins with what seems to be one story, but switches to a parallel-journey story at the end of the setup, when Helen splits into two characters: the one who got on the subway and the one who didn't. The rest of the film follows these two parallel journeys until the end, when the two split characters intersect.

Traffic shows us four parallel journeys: the drug wars in Mexico, the drug czar in Washington, the drug czar's drugged-out daughter, and the wife of the drug dealer in San Diego. Most of the time, these stories continue separately, only occasionally intersecting. *Magnolia* creates nine parallel journeys that are connected by the themes of resolution and redemption.

The Red Violin presents an unusual example of a parallel journey. It's structured with a front story about the auction and the theft of the red violin. This could be said to provide the melody of the story. The film contains two backstories: one about the history of the violin and one that shows a tarot card reading. These stories are the harmonies.

The film's backstories work as recurring motifs, providing a rhythm and harmony of five to ten story beats, almost like a tuba coming in now and then with its boom-boom beat. All of these stories relate to, but don't intersect, the story of the auction. Since these plotlines are separated in time, they have little to do with the major character who steals the violin. Yet, they're an integral part of the story of the violin.

Why did *The Red Violin* work? Because we knew a relationship existed among all of these stories and because the script carefully made the connections clear from scene to scene. Each story reinforced why this violin was worth stealing. We understood the layers, without a writer pounding their interconnectedness into our heads.

Parallel journeys are always in danger of creating a choppy script. Just as one story starts to flow, it's stopped and another starts up. Just as that story starts to flow, it stops so the first one (or a third one) can start up again. And so it goes back and forth—choppy, flowing, choppy, flowing, and so on.

Often, the parallel journeys that start many scripts simply are not necessary. If you're writing a love story, you don't have to introduce the two characters separately. We don't need to know what Harry is doing before meeting Sally or what Sally is doing before meeting Harry. The two can start out together, or we can meet one character through the eyes of the other.

Sometimes, as in films like *Traffic* or *Magnolia*, we're meant to follow the stories separately, expecting that they'll eventually intersect. Then a writer's challenge becomes: How does one introduce each of the parallel stories without creating a choppy script? This comes about through carefully worked-out scene transitions and finding the connecting links among the disparate stories even when it seems there are none. (This will be discussed in more detail in Chapter 3.)

In most parallel-journey stories, we feel that we are moving forward in time. One scene about one character takes place later in time than the previous scene, which was about a different character. Occasionally, however, parallel journeys occur simultaneously.

The French film *Amélie* provides an excellent example of simulataneous parallel journeys that lead to an intersection. We see simultaneous action while a voice-over tells us that at 10:15, Amélie rides the escalator to the metro station. At the same time, the man in red trainers drives his car and looks at a beautiful blonde. Eighteen minutes later, Amélie arrives at the photo booth. At the same moment, the man in the red trainers parks his car in front of the station. A few minutes later, the two meet.

Time Code is another example of simultaneous parallel journeys. The film shows four different stories running simultaneously in four different parts of the screen. Although not commercially successful, this film played with time, implying relationships among its four stories.

The Matrix has a similar parallel-journey structure. In this film, two separate realities play simultaneously, with one in the forefront and the other, which usually remains invisible, moving underneath it on a subtextual level, yet continually influencing the frontstory. In *The Matrix*, the dishonest, inauthentic life is introduced first. This is the world in which Neo lives. When he's offered the chance to see the truth, he moves into the darker, daring, and more authentic reality to fulfill his calling as the savior of that world.

Aside from a few short scenes in which we see the inauthentic life separate from the authentic world, such as when Cypher meets with the agents to betray his team, the film spends most of its time in Neo's new world, with occasional intersections of the two worlds—usually in chase or battle scenes.

The Matrix also contains a third parallel journey that is talked about but never shown: Neo and his group have to save Zion. Yet we never see Zion and know nothing about it. However, this third parallel line influences the other two plotlines, but it's never clear how—so we, the audience, don't fully understand what's at stake. We're certainly rooting for the good guys to win. But the good guys tell us that we're rooting for Zion to survive. What and where is Zion? We never know, so we never have enough information to decide which world we'd choose to save. Intellectually, of course we'd want to choose an authentic and deep reality, but we never get a chance to see what it looks like or to decide if it's worth saving. Although we see the parallel influence of two realities, the third influential storyline, perhaps the most important reality, is invisible.

We can also see the concept of a parallel storyline influencing the major plotline in the film *La Femme Nikita*. Nikita is chosen by a government agent and trained to kill people. There is a reason why Nikita is killing—but we don't know what it is. Presumably, the machinations of the government is the parallel storyline that influences Nikita's actions. Presumably the government had a reason to train her for this work. Presumably the goverment's storyline provides her motivation and the reason for everything that happens. But this storyline remains invisible.

A similar example is found in *Road to Perdition*. The film focuses on the relationship between a gangster, Michael Sullivan, and his son. Implied parallel lines influence this plot, but we rarely see them. We're told that Michael is robbing banks and stealing Al Capone's money, but we never see anything about the Al Capone plotline. We know that Michael's behavior affects another gangster, John Rooney, but John drops out of the film for much of the story, even though he would certainly be adversely affected by Michael's actions. In *Road to Perdition*, at least two parallel-journey plotlines are not played out, as if these other gangsters are non-responsive and on hold while Michael does his action.

These parallel-journey structures can be used to create successful films. But we need to see all the parallel plotlines played out on the screen in order for the structure to work.

THE SPIRAL

The Spiral is a very successful structure for showing character transformation. Although we tend to view our lives as a series of consecutive events, much of our growth is really more like a spiral. We revisit the same themes in our lives. But if we are growing as human beings, each time we come around, we've risen above the problem. We see the theme differently.

We see spiral patterns in such films as *Ordinary People, Prince of Tides,* and *Beloved.* These are psychological stories about remembering an event from the past, coming to terms with it, and resolving it. In these stories, a character revisits a traumatic incident through flashbacks, but each time the incident is revisited, the character is able to remember more or absorb more or deal with it better. The plot keeps spiraling, showing us (and the main character) the same event from a series of different angles. The event from the past is usually played in snippets in Act One and Act Two and played out in its entirety as part of the pay-off in Act Three. This structure's movement is both repetitive and developmental. The story sets up a problem, uses both the present and flashbacks of the past to explore the problem, and then resolves the problem in the third act.

The spiral is one of the few structures in which flashbacks are almost always essential. In this structure, flashbacks are usually precipitated by events that take place on the present-day storyline: Perhaps a psychologist pushes a character to remember a past trauma or certain events in the present remind a character of events from the past. In the spiral form, the climax usually shows the protagonist remembering the entire incident and allowing the past trauma to heal or at least to resolve.

THE UNRAVELING-MYSTERY STRUCTURE

Throughout our lives, we unravel mysteries. Sometimes we try to find answers by reconstructing and reflecting on the past. Agatha Christie used this structure in many of her books, as did the Charlie Chan and Thin Man films. In the classic whodunit stories, a detective is presented with a crime in Act One. In Act Two, he goes about investigating the incident, looking for a perpetrator. In Act Three, the detective adds up the clues and reviews the suspects, finally arriving at a solution, which is then shown through a flashback that depicts the crime being committed.

A complex modern presentation of the unraveling-mystery form is *The Usual Suspects,* which weaves together a story of a heist told from the point of view of a perpetrator who is being interrogated by a detective. We presume that the flashback is the true story, but we learn at the end that things aren't quite what they seem.

When employing this sort of structure, the writer has to be careful not to use obvious third-act exposition in which someone suddenly tells us the truth (like in the old *Perry Mason* TV shows or at the end of *Presumed Innocent*). Instead, a writer needs to lay in clues subtly throughout the film, often using a dramatic third-act reveal—a moment in which we (and the protagonist) suddenly get it. Notice how quickly we unraveled the plot at the end of *The Usual Suspects* once the investigator finally got it. Compare this to the rather clunky unraveling third-act exposition in *Presumed Innocent.*

THE REVERSE STRUCTURE

Some films are structured so that the whole film is a flash-back—beginning at the present and working backward to a key incident from the past. We see this in *Betrayal,* based on the Harold Pinter play of the same name, and in *Memento,* written by Christopher Nolan.

Both of these films use a three-act structure. If their stories were told chronologically, each film's beginning would be the end of its story. The first turning point of the story, if you played it forward, is the second turning point of the story when it's played backward. Both of these films are constructed of individual scenes and sequences. The film flashes back to a scene in the past, then plays out the scene as it moves forward in chronological time. When that scene is over, the story flashes back to a scene that took place before the one we just saw. It plays that one out and then flashes back to one before it, steadily stepping backward in time.

Memento is made up of twenty-five sequences, most of them three to four minutes long (a few slightly longer and a few slightly shorter). The last sequence, which builds to the film's climax, is fourteen minutes long. These sequences are occasionally separated by a short one-minute scene that is usually set in the motel, and usually involves the main character talking on the telephone.

Betrayal is the story of an affair between Emma and Jerry. It is made up of six sequences of varying lengths, ranging from six pages to thirty-seven pages long, showing Emma at the ages of thirty-eight, thirty-six, thirty-four, thirty-two, thirty, and twenty-nine years. At the end, it shows the moment when the two began their affair.

The subject matter of these films is quite different. *Betrayal* is about a relationship, showing how it got to where it is now. *Memento* is the story of a man, Leonard, whose wife was raped and murdered. As a result of this traumatic event, he suffers a rare disease that makes him unable to remember anything for more than a few moments. He tries to find his wife's rapist and murderer by writing notes to himself and taking photos, which act as visual cues to help him "remember" whom he's met, where he's staying, and whom he should trust. He's helped in his investigation by a policeman named Teddy and a woman named Natalie.

The film uses the unraveling-mystery structure as Leonard seeks the truth. But, even when he discovers the truth, he won't be able to remember it.

Both *Betrayal* and *Memento* keep us involved with their back-and-forth motion. The forward motion gives momentum to the the story and moves us forward in our understanding of events, even though the film moves backward in time. Both films also keep us involved by asking compelling questions. The compelling question attached to the reveal of *Memento* is, "What is the truth?" In *Betrayal*, the central question is, "How did they get there?"

Movies that employ a reverse structure are always in danger of confusing us, so a writer has to find ways to keep us oriented. *Memento* keeps us oriented in several ways: It repeats a few lines from the previous scene, so that we clearly understand the connecting links of one scene with another. It uses the props of Leonard's tattoos and photos to show us why, how, and when he took a picture, wrote a sentence, or got a tattoo.

Memento uses a strong three-act structure with well-defined turning points. However, even though a film followed a very tight three-act structure, for me, it really didn't answer its central question: "What is the truth?" Was the truth clear to you at the end? Did the ending confuse you? Did it fascinate you? Did you like its ambiguity? Or did you want clarity from the only truth-teller we had—Teddy?

The Spiral, the Unraveling Mystery, and the Reverse Structure are each designed to get at a truth that is buried in the past. The search in the present and the mystery in the past are integrally connected. The mystery can only be solved by coming to terms with the past, then revealing the truth in the present.

Atlhough these three structures may seem radically different from each other, they each use elements borrowed from traditional storytelling: creating a beginning-middle-end, using scene sequences, asking a central question at the beginning that is answered at the end, and always moving toward a goal or revelation at the climax.

2

A Cinematic Tale
Well Told

Most of the cinematic storytelling patterns I discussed in Chapter 1 reflect our real lives. They reveal our psychology, our themes, the situations in which we find ourselves.

Film stories also deal with patterns that are not based on our real lives, but are based on cinema's inherent possibilities for showing the fantastic. Such stories might be about time machines or altered states of beings that take us to places where no one has gone before. Instead of a linear structure, these inherently cinematic stories are often told through curved structures, such as the circle or the loop. Regardless of the story, the same primary question remains for a writer: What structure best supports the story?

THE CIRCULAR STRUCTURE

In 1995, the Macedonian film *Before the Rain* was nominated for an Academy Award for Best Foreign Film. Its story uses a circular structure to express repeating cycles of violence. The story is told in three parts, with turning points that create a transition from one part to the next.

Part one shows an Albanian girl who runs to a monastery to seek refuge from someone who is trying to kill her. One of the monks helps her escape and tells her that he'll take her to London, where his uncle is a photographer. During the escape, she's killed.

In part two, we meet the photographer, who shows his lover a photo that he took of a dead girl in Macedonia. We recognize the Albanian girl from part one. The photographer later breaks up with his lover, and decides to return home to Macedonia.

In part three, the photographer returns home, where he sees the Albanian girl, who is the daughter of a woman he once loved. Now, the girl is alive. Violence ensues between her and men who threaten her. She escapes and runs to the monastery for help. The end of the film has circled back to the place where it began.

The circle structure is not realistic. In the middle of the film, the girl is both dead and not dead. If you follow the film from the beginning to the middle, it's clear that she died. Not only have we seen it, but there's the photo to prove it. If you go from the end of the film backward to the middle, the girl is alive. We see her alive in part three. So she must have been alive in part two.

The film plays with cinematic truth. It expresses the theme of the circular nature of violence. The cycle goes on and on. The violence keeps repeating without resolution. Men and women and young girls continue to die—again and again.

The film works because each section has direction and movement. Each part has conflict, development, and a beginning, middle, and end. So although we're circling, we still feel as if we're moving forward and as if a film is adding up to a unified whole.

THE LOOPING STRUCTURE

The Looping Structure has a beginning, middle, and end, but it doesn't play them in that order.

A looping structure can be beginning-end-middle, as in *Pulp Fiction*, or it can be the structure of *Mulholland Drive*, which seems to start with the end and then loops back to the beginning and middle and back to the very end.

The looping structure is not the same as the reverse structure (discussed in Chapter 1), which starts at the end and moves to the middle and then to the beginning. Instead, the looping structure plays around with the ordering of events, showing relationships and transformations that wouldn't be clear if using a linear structure.

Although one could analyze *Pulp Fiction* as a four-act structure, I'm going to analyze it as a three-act structure since Act One and Act Three so clearly fit into a traditional three-act structure.

The story begins and ends with a scene that acts as a frame. Two robbers decide to hold up a restaurant. The credits then begin, and this scene is left behind to be picked up again toward the end of Act Three.

In Act One, Vincent and Jules are sent by their boss, Marsellus, to kill three young men who have betrayed him. They kill two of them, not knowing that the third one is hiding in the bathroom.

In the first half of Act Two, Vincent takes Marsellus' wife, Mia, out on a date, because Marsellus asked him to take care of her while he's gone. On the date, she almost dies of a drug overdose. Vincent and Mia decide not to talk about the incident.

At the film's midpoint, a character presents a young boy, Butch, with his father's watch, telling him that his father saved this watch for him while he was a prisoner of war.

In the second half of Act Two, Butch, who has grown up to become a boxer, is asked by Marsellus to throw a fight. He doesn't. Instead, Butch kills his opponent and escapes with his ditzy girlfriend, killing Vincent as he tries to get away. Before Butch can leave town, he and Marsellus meet on the street, are captured, overcome their captors, and barely escape with their lives.

In Act Three, we return to the killing scene of Act One. We now enter the scene just when the man hiding in the bathroom comes out, shooting, but misses both Vincent and Jules. Jules considers this a miracle, so it becomes a transforming experience. Vincent and Jules capture the shooter, but Vincent's gun accidentally goes off, killing the young man and making a big bloody mess in the car. They turn to Marsellus for help, and he sends The Wolf over to help them clean up and get rid of all the evidence. At the end, Vincent and Jules go to a restaurant to celebrate and get caught up in the film's framing scene—the robbery that we saw before the opening credits rolled.

If we placed *Pulp Fiction's* events in chronological order, we'd see Act One, Act Three, Act Two. Act Three loops back to the middle.

The looping structure is used partly to clarify Jules' transformation. The robbery frame and Act One and Act Three focus on Jules' story. If a traditional beginning-middle-end structure had been used, Jules would have dropped out of the story in Act One, since he quits working for Marsellus after the "miracle." Vincent would have dropped out of the story in Act Two, since he's killed by Butch and Butch's story continues after Vincent's death in the second half of Act Two.

Although *Pulp Fiction* seems, at a quick glance, to defy traditional notions of structure, it actually achieves its success by using a stronger structure than most films.

It uses two frames. The restaurant robbery frame, which begins and ends the film, works like a bookend, holding the film together. A second frame, Vincent's and Jules' confrontation with Marsellus' betrayers, which is the second scene in the film and returns in Act Three, forms a frame within a frame, connecting Act One and Act Three. This film is very clever in its use of this second frame. Generally, a frame is a film's first scene and last scene, like the restaurant robbery. However, the second frame, the confrontation of the betrayers, doesn't come back at the *end* of Act Three, but at the *beginning* of Act Three. The frames are unusual but effective. They give a tight structure to the film, holding its disparate parts together.

Pulp Fiction gives each of its loosely connected stories a three-act structure, and each plays out strong scene sequences:

- Mia's story of her date with Vincent has a beginning-middle-end.
- Butch's boxing story has a beginning-middle-end.
- Vincent's story has a beginning-middle-end.
- Jules' story had a beginning-middle-end.

Each of these stories uses action and movement to reach its goals.

In my own experience consulting with non-linear structures, I find that I need to very tightly structure them to keep the stories from breaking up and flying in a hundred different directions. Non-linear stories can easily become episodic, go off on tangents, and seem disconnected. Strong, solid structuring can help hold a non-linear form together and keep us connected with its multiple stories, which may seem, on the surface, to have only tenuous connections with one another.

Although the looping structure is something of a rarity, in 2001 it was used in *Mulholland Drive,* which was one of the most talked-about films of that year. Critics raved about it, but then mentioned that they didn't understand it. Whoopi Goldberg joked at the Academy Awards that the awards ceremony would be long, but not as long as it takes to explain *Mulholland Drive.*

Mulholland Drive was nominated for an Academy Award for Best Director. Although it was not nominated for Best Picture or Best Screenplay, it's an important film to analyze, in terms of what worked and why it worked and what didn't work, and what might have been done about it.

The film's structure is made up of two unequal parts: The first section lasts for approximately 116 minutes and recounts the story of a young actress, Betty, who comes to Hollywood, stays at her aunt's apartment, befriends a woman with amnesia named Rita, auditions for acting roles, falls in love with Rita, and helps Rita discover her own identity.

The second part, which lasts about twenty-eight minutes, shows a washed-out actress named Diane (who is played by the same actress who plays Betty in the film's first section). She is in love with the very successful actress Camilla (who is played by the same actress who plays Rita in the first section). Their relationship is disintegrating, and out of her despair, Diane hires a hitman to kill Camilla. At the end, Diane has a psychotic episode and commits suicide.

Every reviewer seems to agree that the film did not work as a cohesive whole.

Roger Ebert loved it, but couldn't explain any of it. He says it's all a dream. This is a different interpretation than many other reviewers who see the last twenty-eight minutes as reality, and the first section as a dream or a psychotic episode.

Stephen Holden, writing in *The New York Times*, saw it as being about the allure of Hollywood and multiple role-playing, rather than about any single character (even though Betty is clearly the protagonist). He sees it as surrealistic and being about our ability to move in and out of dreams.

Others, such as some of my acting friends in the industry, felt it was a critique of Hollywood, which often forces directors to cast those they don't want and uses up, eats up, and spits out talent.

Others see it as about desperation, and how those in Hollywood will do anything to get a role and become famous.

Unfortunately, every one of the aforementioned interpretations has flaws. No matter how one looks at this film, some scenes don't make sense and some episodes and characters don't fit.

Three reviewers—Max Garrone, Andy Klein, and Bill Wyman, writing on salon.com—decided to take the whole film apart and try to figure it out. They believed that the first 116 minutes is a story that Diane constructed after she hired the hitman. According to this interpretation, the beginning and middle of a film, its first two acts, progress chronologically. But they take place sometime *during* the events of Act

Three, when a desperate Diane decides to hire a hitman. When Diane realizes the evil she's done by trying to kill Camilla (who may or may not have escaped this assassination attempt), she replays part of her life (Act One and Act Two of a film), but this time casts herself as the loving, kind, and happy Betty, who is helping Rita find her identity. This interpretation holds that Diane has constructed this story as a result of her guilt over hiring the hitman and as an expression of her developing psychosis.

This interpretation seems to make the most sense to me. If it's accurate, most of the last 28-minute section of the film actually happens before the events of a film's first 116 minutes. So the story begins with the psychosis shown in Act Three, and then loops back to how she got to this point, playing out a film's beginning and middle, which is all in Diane's imagination, and then loops to a story's very end, when she commits suicide.

If you were mesmerized and pulled in by the story, this was partly because the film structured each of its small stories to have a beginning-middle-end and a goal. Betty arrives in Hollywood, practices, and gets an audition, where she wows the producer and fellow actors. The director meets with his producers, resists their casting requirements, but then casts who they want. Rita arrives at Betty's and tries to find out who she is with Betty's help. Each of these characters has a clear desire, which they follow throughout each of these segments.

Each section uses scene sequences that give the film forward movement and a sense of cohesiveness, even though the film as a whole is not cohesive. Scene sequences include: Rita almost being killed but then escaping; Adam getting fired from his directing job and then rehired; Adam going home to find his wife in bed with the gardener; Betty trying to get an acting job and getting an audition; Betty meeting and falling in love with Rita; Betty hiring a hitman.

Each of these stories has a sense of mystery about it. If you were mesmerized by a film, it was partly because the mystery within each section kept pulling you in. You wondered where it would lead. Like *Memento*, you probably asked, "What is the truth?" The confusing nature of the film was not due to meandering stories, but because the sum of its parts and the meaning of the whole film is unclear.

If we think about film as communication as well as expression, then a film can be judged by whether it successfully communicates an idea. The more difficult the idea is to communicate, the more a film needs clear and understandable scenes that ground the audience so it doesn't get lost. This doesn't mean talking down to the audience, or being so obvious that all artistry is lost, but it does mean helping the audience find moments of orientation that will lead it to an understanding of what a filmmaker wants to communicate.

In *Mulholland Drive*, a number of scenes could have been set up to ground the audience. We learn toward the end of the film that Betty came to Hollywood because she won a jitterbug contest. She believed her dancing qualified her for stardom. The film opens with a jitterbug contest, but we never see Betty dancing. We see a brunette dancing at the beginning—but not Betty/Diane. So the first opportunity to ground us in Betty's or Diane's situation is not used.

Following this dance contest is a closeup of a red comforter or a red pillow. Might this be the beginning of a dream or the beginning of a real story? Or is it an arbitrary image that Lynch chose to add? We don't know, and there are no connecting links with this image to help us understand it.

Throughout the film, the director is told to cast Camilla Rhodes in his new picture. He's shown a photo of Camilla, and we see someone named Camilla sing, although this is not the woman we will come to know as Camilla/Rita. So the Camilla in the middle of a film is not the same Camilla we find at the end of a film. This confusion kills any chance of the audience becoming grounded with this character.

When Betty and Rita visit Diane's apartment, a neighbor tells them that she hasn't seen Diane for a few days, and that

Diane has some of her stuff, which she'll be right over to collect. Rita and Betty go into Diane's apartment and immediately smell something—the dead Diane. They hear the neighbor's knocking. And then we see a closeup of a decomposed body that must have been dead for more than a few days.

At a film's second turning point, we hear Diane's neighbor knocking again, and the body that we believe to be dead gets out of bed to answer the door. We see it's Diane. Instead of telling Diane that she hasn't seen her for a few days (as in the earlier Betty/Rita story), the neighbor tells her she hasn't seen her for a few weeks. Here was a chance to ground us by using a consistent time line—but now three weeks have passed instead of three days, and Diane is alive, not dead.

One might ask if this film's primary problem is a structural one or a stylistic one. It's both. The looping structure may not have been the best choice to convey these particular illusions and psychoses. When Betty's story is told for the first 116 minutes, it has a certain logic to it. If this was meant to be a psychotic or dream episode, it's far too linear to convey the dream-state's process. If this is meant to be a dream of a psychotic episode, it doesn't stay within Betty's point of view. It tells us side stories. We might wonder why these stories would be so important to the self-involved Betty. Although we might understand why Betty could imagine Adam being forced to cast Camilla instead of her, it's less clear why Betty would want to concoct a side story about the director and his wife, who's having an affair with the gardener.

The idea of playing out the story of a good girl who we later see is not a good girl is a fine idea. But very few clues connect the good-girl and bad-girl stories. We could have been grounded by insights into Betty's point of view, helping us understand how her mind worked. But many scenes don't give us any insight into her point of view. We move back and forth, from seeing Betty's version of events to pulling back to an objective reality. So the protagonist's reality, which may be the last twenty-eight minutes of a film, doesn't help the audience understand a film.

Maybe David Lynch wanted us to first experience psychosis and then experience the reality from which it grew, but by setting up the abnormal state first, reviewers and audiences were confused. Although he could have created transition scenes to help us understand his idea behind the story and the structure, he chose not to.

Many reviewers commented that Lynch probably did not want us to understand his movie (a rather strange stance for a filmmaker to take). Loose threads and disconnected parts abound, whether it's the detective who is in both the psychotic story and the true story or the confusion of subjective and objective stories or the question of whether the hitman was really incompetent or what *really* happened and who was the scary man behind the wall.

If you loved the movie, you no doubt submerged yourself in its mystery and its incoherent and disparate parts. But you should be aware that it's not a model that will lead you to better writing. If you only liked parts of the movie, perhaps you can use those parts as models for constructing something that has a hidden inner logic.

When working with confusing mental processes, a writer has to continually ground the audience. *A Beautiful Mind* also dealt with mental illness, but it kept the audience grounded in its story by sometimes showing us the story through John Nash's point of view, but then pulling back to allow us to see it through the points of view of his wife, his psychiatrist, and his fellow mathematicians. As a result, by the film's end, we had no doubt about the reality and the truth that the story was conveying.

PLAYING WITH CINEMATIC TIME

Only rarely does a film play out a story in real time. The last 100 minutes of *Titanic* were done in the 100 minutes that it took for the ship to sink. The last act of *Goodfellas* conveyed a real-time situation.

Most films take place in a fairly short period of time, which is meant to convey the idea of real time. Some films depict events that take place over one night or one day (the *Die Hard* films, *High Noon*) or over a period of a few days (*Three Days of the Condor, Titanic*) or a few weeks to a few months (*Adaptation, American Beauty, The Sixth Sense, Shakespeare in Love*) or around a year (*The Fugitive, Erin Brockovich*). Sometimes a story's progression from one scene to the next jumps time by hours, days, weeks, or even years. Generally, the shorter the period of time depicted, the more intense the drama.

The longer the period of time depicted in a film, the more chance there is that its narrative line will become episodic, making it more difficult to keep the film flowing. If a film takes place over a long period of time, it needs to find ways to keep the story moving and cohesive. *Driving Miss Daisy* moves through twenty-five years. It shows this vast period of time by changing the seasons, changing the calendar, changing the models of the cars. It keeps the story moving by playing scene sequences within these various time periods.

Some films play with time travel, such as the *Back to the Future* stories. Other films play with two different temporal realities. In *Red,* by Polish director Krzysztof Kieslowski, we discover that the timeline of the story we watch for most of the film eventually intersects with a timeline in the past. At that moment, the story brings together two people from two different time periods—which is impossible, except in the world of cinematic reality.

In *Frequency,* a father and son talk to each other, even though they live thirty years apart. Although this film was not very effective because its inner logic didn't always hold it together, it did show another way of playing with time.

In *Schindler's List,* scenes are sometimes intercut so that they *seem* to be in the same time period, but are not. Toward the beginning of the film, after Schindler has started his factory, a one-armed man comes to thank him for saving his life. In the next part of this scene sequence, workers arrive at work in the morning, with the happy one-armed man singing. They're stopped by the Nazis and are required to shovel snow. At this point, the film cuts to a scene that shows Schindler complaining to the commandant about his workers shoveling snow. When the Nazis notice how very ineffective the one-armed man is, they take him out and shoot him. The next scene moves back to Schindler and the commandant, showing Schindler complain about the loss of a worker.

Watching this scene, we might think that Schindler and the commandant are somewhere near the workers, maybe even watching them shovel snow, since Schindler looks out the window at one point. But it's clear by the end of the scene that both scenes with the commandant happened at the same time, sometime after the snow-shoveling scene. We accept the intercutting of scenes and the differences in time, because they're connected by being part of the same episode.

Schindler's List uses a similar technique several other times. When Schindler is drawing up a list of people to be saved, the scene is intercut with various scenes of Schindler trying to talk others into helping the Jews. Clearly these intercut scenes are not going on at the same time, but the list that Schindler is working on unites these scenes from different periods of time.

The Hours shows us three different time periods: 1921, 1951, and 2001 (with a very short section set in the 1940s). Although these are clearly separate timelines, we sense that the story Virginia Woolf is writing in the 1920s is determining events in the future.

In the Mexican film, *Tu Mamá También,* we hear about past, present, and future time. Sometimes, as the main characters drive through the countryside, the narrator tells us that an accident happened in this same place five years ago. Or, as we meet the fisherpeople, the narrator tells us what will happen to them in the future. The technique is interesting, but it's *telling* us about time rather than *showing* us. And, most of the time, this information is not directly relevant to the context or theme or primary storyline.

When playing with time, you can connect the different time periods by carrying objects through from one time period to another: the flowers and the book in *The Hours,* the window and the list in *Schindler's List,* the car in *Back to the Future.* Disparate parts often will feel connected if we see some of the same objects in different time periods.

EXPERIMENTING, AND MAKING IT WORK

Once a writer has determined the best structure for his or her story, the entire script must be created in an organic way so that the story hangs together. We've all seen films that were wonderful *until* something happened that caused the story to swerve off course or become muddled—almost as if the writer and director didn't know how to balance all the dramatic elements to keep the story cohesive. As a result, the audience may feel frustrated and unsatisfied.

Films so many times lose their focus when they move off of a linear structure that one could easily say that we must, therefore, only use linear structures. This is limiting. It limits us as artists who want to find new forms, and it limits us as human beings who reflect on life and realize that some stories we want to tell don't fit neatly into nice beginnings, middles, and ends.

How do we explore non-linear structures and still maintain a cohesive script? We do it partly by recognizing that every time we move away from a linear arrangement of events, we need to compensate in some way for the dramatic elements that don't fall neatly into place. To know when, where, and how to compensate for this, we need to understand traditional three-act structures so well that we can begin to play with them. Building on the past is the most natural means of growth.

Just as Schoenberg learned his traditional harmony long before he created his twelve-tone music and Picasso learned to draw before he created cubism, screenwriters must also learn the craft of writing before they can experiment. They need to develop both conscious and intuitive feelings for what works and what doesn't work. They need to care as much about clarity and communication as they do about personal expression and their artistic voice. They need to be willing to be on an artistic quest that asks questions such as:

- How do I find a structure that conveys and supports my story?
- How do I keep the audience engaged and clear about what I'm trying to communicate?
- How can I work with the traditional elements of scriptwriting and still find new patterns and new ways of telling a story?
- How do I find new techniques that will ensure that whatever structure I use will not be choppy or confusing? How do I keep my story moving and focused?

3

Keep It
Moving, Moving, Moving

A writer is like an architect who designs a house, knowing it will collapse if the relationship of its parts is unbalanced. A writer is like a composer who strives for the sweep and soar of the music, while paying attention to each individual measure, knowing the change of even one note can either enhance or diminish the entire piece. Like a jeweler grouping beautiful gems for a splendid necklace, a writer must pay attention to each individual scene, as well as the way it connects to the scenes that surround it. The screenwriter strives to create a script that feels as if it is all of one piece. It mustn't feel pasted together, as if a writer grabbed something from here and something from there. It mustn't feel like a string of individual stories from disparate sources.

A script is about relationships: relationships between characters, relationships between the plot and subplot lines, relationships between themes and images, relationships between individual scenes. A writer sees a forest, and then a large group of trees, and then a smaller group, and finally an individual tree—an individual scene. Or some writers might begin with individual trees, and then build a forest. Either way, to create a cohesive and integrated script, a writer moves back and forth between working with the story as a whole and working with its small details. A writer carefully plans a script's many relationships, by strategizing the rise and fall of the action, variety in pacing, smooth scene transitions, and the overall forward momentum of the story.

A story has to move. It has to go somewhere. It advances toward its climax. How does a writer keep the story moving from scene to scene?

In linear storytelling, this movement often comes naturally. The story simply flows because it has a strong catalyst at the beginning and a clear goal that provides a track that implies which scenes naturally follow and how each scene is connected to the others. The more complicated a script's structure, the more attention a writer has to pay to how the individual scenes and scene sequences are constructed.

USING A CLEAR NARRATIVE LINE TO CREATE A COHESIVE SCRIPT

A cohesive script is held together by its many carefully constructed elements. When viewed as a whole, these form a thread by which most (if not all) scenes advance the story. A script has movement because one scene implies the next or may even imply an entire sequence of subsequent scenes. A narrative line is set when a character states an intention—overtly or subtly. Once an intention is stated, it implies action.

At the first turning point of *The Fugitive* (approximately twenty-five minutes into a film), Sam Gerard announces that the fugitive's name is Dr. Richard Kimble. He tells his deputies, "Go get him." This statement lays down the film's narrative line. We know what Sam wants. We know his intention and his goal. The statement also implies action. We expect investigations and chases and wrong turns and plenty of action in Act Two. Every scene in Act Two and Act Three is somehow related to the cat-and-mouse plot that begins with Gerard's command.

Once a character's intention is set forth, as long as a writer doesn't allow the story to get off track, the story will move forward. That track most certainly doesn't negate the need for variety, surprises, turns, twists—that's where originality and talent come in—but it does give the script a definite track to follow.

CREATING THE SCENE SEQUENCE

Writers don't just construct scenes but sequences of scenes. Just as each scene has a focus, so does each scene sequence. If a writer views scenes in their larger context—as groups of scenes rather than as individual scenes—and designs a script accordingly, a writer will find it easier to create cohesiveness and a narrative flow throughout a script. By linking individual scenes into a scene sequence, the script stays focused.

When I consult, I often put titles to scene groupings to make sure that each grouping has its own focus. In *Lord of the Rings*, I might title the sequences: The Warning, Preparation for Leaving, Moving Through the Valley, Fighting the Orcs, The Great Escape, etc.

Schindler's List contains scene sequences that could be titled The Jews Are Forced into the Ghetto (four-minute sequence), The Ghetto Massacre (sixteen-minute sequence), Goeth Tries to Be Good (thirteen-minute sequence), and Moving Schindler's Workers to Czechoslovakia (twenty-three-minute sequence). Each individual scene is related to the focus of the scene sequence in which it appears. If you watch The Ghetto Massacre sequence, you'll notice that every scene is related to this massacre. If you watch the Czechoslovakia sequence, you'll notice that every one of its scenes relates to Schindler's intention to move his factory workers.

Each scene sequence should develop toward a climax. In *Lord of the Rings*, the Preparation for Leaving sequence reaches its climax when Frodo leaves, and then the next sequence begins. In *Schindler's List*, the Goeth Tries to Be Good sequence develops to its climax when he shoots the boy.

CREATING ACTION-REACTION LINKS BETWEEN SCENES

One of the best ways to create movement from one scene to the next is to imply an action at the end of one scene that is then carried out in the following scene. I call this an action-reaction sequence. Basically it compresses time, jumping us forward. This is one of the most effective and time-tested methods to keep a story moving. Probably every film since the beginning of the film industry has used this technique.

In one scene in *Traffic*, Salazar asks Francisco to inform. The scene ends with Francisco beginning to write down a list of names. The next scene shows Manolo and Javier finding the men from this list. In scene #115, Javier tells Anna that he'll find her husband. Then in scene #116, he does. In scene #184, Francisco is shot, but he doesn't know who shot him. Then in scene #185 we see a strange man packing up a rifle.

In *Fargo*, Marge gets a call to investigate a murder. In the next scene, she checks out the crime scene. In one scene in *The Piano*, Ada asks Baines to help her bring back her piano. In the next scene, he does.

Sometimes films don't flow because a scene ends on a static note instead of setting up the action to follow. In *Traffic*, when Barbara (wife) and Caroline (daughter) congratulate Robert on his new appointment as drug czar, Caroline's line ends the scene: "It's great, daddy. It's just amazing, that's all." The next scene then moves to the San Diego story.

Notice how this drug-czar scene ends with a statement rather than a question or a demand or an intention. It stops the story. It doesn't imply development, or action, or any connecting link with any scenes that may follow.

Sometimes transitions are choppy because an implied scene is not played out. At the end of scene #55, Gordon says, "We have a warrant to search your home, Mrs. Ayala," thereby implying action.

It's a perfect setup for the next scene in this sequence. It wouldn't be necessary to play the obvious "searching the home" scene, although there'd be nothing wrong with doing that. But it does imply a scene. Instead, the script *cuts to* the Mexican story and we never see the house searched.

You might want to re-watch *Traffic* to see where it moves and where it doesn't. It's a good script to study for momentum. I admire the script and the film for its richness and ability to work with parallel stories, but find that the film doesn't always solve the major challenges in parallel-journey stories: keeping the flow and momentum going when the storylines are not intrinsically connected.

THE DELAYED RESPONSE

When a reaction scene is delayed, it can keep audiences alert and keep a story moving. In *Traffic*, at the end of scene #144, Carlos tells his wife, Helena, to look at a particular painting that hangs in their home. This scene implies the question, "What's the importance of the painting?" Six scenes later, she checks the painting and discovers an envelope behind it containing valuable information.

In scene #140, Robert tells his daughter that she must get help for her drug addiction. She says, "You can't make me" and he answers, "Oh, yes I can." Five scenes later, we see the reaction scene—Caroline is at Serenity Oaks Treatment Facility.

Delayed reaction scenes never provide as much momentum as action-reaction sequences, but *Traffic* used them well to keep us connected to its multiple stories. We anticipated a reaction and were willing to wait for it.

LINKING SCENES BY USING SIMILARITIES

One of the most common techniques for linking scenes is to cut from an object in one scene to a similar object in the next scene. Perhaps a telephone rings and then, in the next scene, someone picks up the receiver.

Sometimes the prop in one scene is not related to the prop in another, but the similarities in appearance or use implies a connection. Perhaps the scene-to-scene cut is from a mirror to a window. Or a murderer might pick up a knife in one scene, and then CUT TO a chef chopping vegetables. The chef might be a character in a love story subplot who has absolutely no relationship with either the murderer or the victim. The similarity of props can make us feel a connection between two scenes that may not be otherwise related.

Sometimes the scene-to-scene cuts are created by the director or editor. In *Dead Poets Society*, director Peter Weir saw a relationship between the pattern of birds flying in the sky and the pattern of the boys running down the stairs to their classes. He and the editor placed the striking images of two scenes next to each other as a link. However, most of the times, these cuts are worked out by the screenwriter.

The Hours uses cuts from one similar image to another similar image to connect its different stories. These cuts may be from flowers in one scene to flowers in the next or from a sleeping woman to a sleeping woman or from Virgina writing a book to Laura reading that book or from someone leaving at the end of one scene to someone leaving at the beginning of the next scene.

Magnolia sometimes links scenes through the use of similar props. Scene #260 ends with liquid morphine dripping into Earl's mouth. Scene #261 begins with Claudia looking at the coke in front of her, and then snorting it. The link of these two different drugs forms a connection between the two characters, both in need of redemption. In scene #54, Donnie runs into the glass window of a 7-Eleven. In the next scene, Phil enters Earl's home carrying coffee in a 7-Eleven cup.

All scripts contain inherent connections between scenes. These connections might include a cut from a moving object in one scene to a different moving object in the next scene. Or a filmmaker may cut from a door opening in one scene to a door closing in the next scene.

Sometimes a film doesn't play these inherent connections. Due to a lack of these connections, I experienced a choppiness in the cuts from scene to scene in *Traffic,* especially in the beginning of a film. Although the choppiness may seem organic to a storyline that plays disparate multiple storylines, a number of scenes implied connections between them that could have been played, to help the scenes connect and flow. Early in a film, one scene ends with a car driving. The next scene begins with a building exterior, and then shows a car moving into the driveway. The obvious cut was car to car. But either consciously or unconsciously, the filmmaker made the choice not to play this connection. Scene #35 ends with cocaine spilling out of a van. The next scene begins by showing teenagers in a guest house listening to music and TV, and then we see that they're taking drugs. The connecting link here is the drugs. But the scene did not move from drugs to drugs, which could have created more flow to the story.

You may want to re-watch this film and see where you feel it's choppy and where you feel it flows, and see if you can identify the techniques that made the difference.

CREATING MOMENTUM THROUGH CONTRASTS

Sometimes a cut is used for the purpose of contrast so that we see a connection between scenes through their opposition to one another. This might be a cut from one contrasting mood to another. Perhaps one scene is placed at night in the gritty streets of New York where a murder is taking place. CUT TO the inside of a cathedral where a sweet-faced choir is singing and all seems right with the world. Or cut from city to country or from dark to light. Like life, which is full of surprising contrasts, these juxtapositions keep a film fresh, fascinating, and intriguing.

Sometimes a contrasting cut is used to create tension and horror: "Nothing can go wrong now," says the strong, protective man to the woman in jeopardy. CUT TO the monster at the window.

Occasionally a cut from one scene to the next contradicts something that is said or done. While the audience sees the contradiction, the characters may not. In *Secret & Lies*, when Hortense first calls Cynthia to tell her that Cynthia is her birth mother, Cynthia doesn't want to talk to her. Hortense asks if she would take down her number anyway, and Cynthia says, "Oh, I don't think I've got a pencil." Then, CUT TO Cynthia on the phone, holding a ballpoint pen in her hand. That cut gives us a great deal of information about Cynthia and her emotional confusion.

In the first *Godfather*, there are intercutting scenes between the baptism scene and the murder spree. And in *The Godfather: Part III*, there are intercuts between the murders and the opera.

UNDERSTANDING THE INFORMATION BETWEEN CUTS

Most cuts imply information or action that is taking place off-screen between the cuts. At the first turning point of *Tootsie*, Michael decides to prove his agent wrong when the agent tells him that no one will hire him. Off-screen, he puts on a dress, prepares for the try-out, and goes to the television studio. In the next scene we see the consequences of Michael's off-screen action—he has the job and is now Dorothy Michaels.

In *Schindler's List*, Schindler tries to figure out how to move his workers to a safe place in Czechoslovakia. He knows he needs Goeth's permission to do it. And he knows the way to get his permission is with money.

```
                    SCHINDLER
          All you have to do is tell me
          what it's worth to you.
          What's a person worth to you?
```

```
Goeth thinks about it in silence. Then
slowly nods to himself. He's going to make
some money out of this even if he can't
figure it out. He smiles.

                    GOETH
      What's one worth to you?
      That's the question.

                                        CUT TO:

THE KEYS OF A TYPEWRITER slapping a
name onto a list.
I T Z H A K    S T E R N - the letters the
size of buildings, the sound as loud as
gunshots.
```

Off-screen, between the scenes, Schindler has obviously made the decision to purchase his workers' safety.

Sometimes the information between scenes is humorous. It's as if the one scene presents a joke setup and the next one presents the punchline. One of my favorite cuts comes from *The People vs. Larry Flynt*. Flynt says, "I got to move somewhere where perverts are welcome." The audience may unconsciously ask the question, Where might that be? The next scene provides the answer: CUT TO the Hollywood sign.

CREATING CONNECTIONS THROUGH MUSIC AND WORDPLAY

Magnolia is particularly skillful at linking scenes that seem unrelated to each other. For most of the film, the narrative line is unclear. The film is not held together by its storyline. And there is no character that holds all the storylines together. A central idea is not readily apparent for most of the film. Not until its end are the connections between characters apparent.

Much of this film's action is played against a strong musical score, and many diverse scenes are played with the *same* musical background. Although, at times, I found that the music called too much attention to itself, it did provide a link between scenes. In *Magnolia*, each character sings a verse of the song "It's Not Going to Stop." The song plays over various scenes—Claudia snorting coke in her apartment, Jim getting dressed in his apartment, Jimmy Gator sitting in his office, Donnie Smith in his apartment, Phil at Earl's house, Linda in the parking lot, Frank in his car, Stanley in the library.

Sometimes this film uses words to link scenes. In scene #155, the Whiz Kids are given a musical bonus question, and the answer is "Carmen." The love song from *Carmen* plays over the following scene in which Kurring and Claudia are beginning their relationship. This music resonates with a theme of love as we see scenes that show Donnie's yearning for love, Frank's lack of love, and Linda's love for her husband.

Sound can be used to bridge one scene to another. In *Howard's End*, Margaret confronts Henry about his affair with Jackie. As they begin to talk about it, the scene goes to black. We hear the ticking of a clock, and then the scene continues, as if it is some minutes or perhaps hours later. During this scene, there are two blackouts that show the passage of time. You'll notice that one has the ticking of a clock, the other is silent. The ticking of the clock forms a good connection between the scene on either side of the blackouts. The silent cut is less successful and looks as if the projector had broken for a few seconds.

WHAT CAN GO WRONG WITH TRANSITIONS?

Sometimes, in a zealous attempt to create a strong narrative flow, a writer or filmmaker tries to create scene-to-scene connections where none exist. In some of Steven Spielberg's films from the 1980s, when he was moving from being a popular filmmaker to being a more artistic filmmaker, he created some very strange transitions in his efforts to force connections. In *The Color Purple*, some of his cuts were heavy-handed and contrived. (And I believe that these heavy-handed transitions were the work of the director, not the screenwriter, since they weren't organic to the story.) In the scene when Celie leaves Mister, she looks down from the train to the railroad tracks as the train moves faster and faster, and the tracks become blacker and blacker. Then CUT TO the black interior of a mailbox. This seems to be forcing a connection when there is none. Although from black to black shows a creative mind that can see connections when there are few, nevertheless, it felt over the top to me.

Cuts from scene to scene are not meant to be arbitrary. They need to be well thought out to give a story focus and movement and clarity. A writer should not try to contrive connections, but instead seek intrinsic connections between scenes. Later the director and editor will build on the transitions the writer has suggested.

CREATING A THREAD TO HOLD YOUR STORY TOGETHER

Sometimes a script is pulled together by a thread that weaves its way through the script. In some linear scripts and most non-linear scripts, the threads that keeps the story focused do not come from the stories themselves, but from somewhere else. Sometimes a character holds the story together.

Creating a thread with a character

In some scripts, this thread comes from a character who moves through the script. This is particularly important in a script such as *Pulp Fiction,* in which there seem to be three different stories. How did writers Roger Avery and Quentin Tarantino connect this film's disparate parts? Through the character of Marsellus.

Marsellus is the common denominator in all three stories: the story of Marsellus' young betrayers whom Vincent and Jules were sent to punish; the story of the boxer, Butch, who threw the match Marsellus tried to fix; the story of Vincent's date with Mia, Marsellus' wife. In each of these stories, Marsellus is the controlling influence. He is the adversary. If the characters do not follow his wishes, they will be punished or killed. If we were to ever forget that Marsellus is the thread, the story would feel arbitrary. But throughout the film, just when the audience might forget him, he appears again.

In *Magnolia*, Earl Partridge is a common-denominator character. Although he is not a clear link among all the stories, he links Frank's story, Linda's story, and Phil's story, and provides a thematic link with the other stories—all of which are about people seeking reconciliation.

Magnolia also uses additional character-based links, showing the similarities among various characters' situations. The film has two cancer stories: the father, Earl, and the husband, Jimmy Gator. It has several love stories: Linda's love for her husband, Jim Kurring's developing relationship with Claudia, Frank's lack of love, Phil's care for Earl.

Creating a thread with an idea

In *Traffic*, the thread is its theme and subject matter. Connecting various parts of a story through an idea presents a special problem, because ideas are vague, philosophical, and potentially intellectual. You can't see or feel an idea. A writer may have difficulty finding concrete ways to show ideas on the screen, rather than talking about ideas. Of course, in the case of *Traffic*, drugs are specific, and we can see them, but *Traffic* is not mainly about taking drugs or moving drugs (as are movies like *Rush, Panic in Needle Park, Trainspotting, Drugstore Cowboy*) but about the relationship between the corruption and/or incompetence found at the root of its four drug-related stories.

Traffic does not begin with a story. It begins with four situations: drug dealing in Mexico, drug buying in San Diego, kids taking drugs in the United States, and America's new drug czar trying to figure out how to do his job well. The "War on Drugs" will address all of these issues and their relationships with each other.

These four different situations are first presented as parallel journeys, and each develops toward a climax. As the film proceeds, they begin to intersect, but only marginally as stories. However, they all have a simlar theme that explores widespread corruption, showing the relationship of the theme to four different aspects of the drug trade.

Creating a thread with an object

Sometimes a film's connecting thread is a prop that moves throughout the story. In *The Red Violin*, the violin provides the thread that connects the tarot-card reader from one century, the beautiful woman from another century, and the man who wants the violin for his son.

In *Pulp Fiction*, the midpoint introduces a watch that has been passed on to Butch by his father. The watch serves as a connecting link between the midpoint and the second half of a film. The importance of this watch provides the motivation for all the risks that Butch takes to escape from Marsellus. It becomes the motor for the second half of Act Two, and it connects Butch with Vincent, who guards Butch's apartment and is killed when Butch returns for his watch.

Magnolia uses weather information as a bridge between scenes, using the prop of a title card to present the weather report. In the third act of *Magnolia*, frogs rain on all the characters.

In *Forrest Gump*, the feather and chocolates thread their way throughout a film, pulling its disparate parts together to create a sense of a cohesive whole.

Creating a thread with place

Sometimes, all the characters in a story have ties to a single location, even though their individual stories may seem unrelated to each other. Two people in the same place at the same time will seem connected, even though that connection may be minimal.

In *Magnolia*, the television quiz show acts as a bridge to connect characters who seem unrelated to each other. The quiz show plays on television in the background of various scenes—Claudia snorting coke in her apartment, Jim in his apartment getting dressed, Jimmy Gator sitting in his office, Donnie Smith in his apartment, Phil at Earl's house, Linda at the drug store, Frank in his car, and Stanley in the library.

In *Magnolia,* the fluid rhythm of the camera also links scenes that take place in different locations. The camera seems to wander from story to story as it travels from the room of one character to a room of a different character who might live miles away. The cuts from scene to scene sometimes make it look as if we were in the same place: The camera goes around the corner of one room and then around the corner of another room in a different location. Sometimes the camera moved through the doorway of one location and then cuts to the doorway of another.

Traffic occasionally created intersections of two of its stories by allowing characters from differnt stories to be in the same location, even if only for a moment. The first intersection occurs in scene #61. In the San Diego story, Helena leaves the jail where her husband is incarcerated for selling drugs, gets into her car, and drives through a shopping district in San Diego as Javier and Manolo are walking down the same street. The film then follows Javier and Manolo as they go into a bar to meet an informer, Francisco. Javier and Helena also intersect in scene #213, when they both drive across the Mexican border.

Just as the careful construction of scene sequences and scene transitions are important, so is the careful construction and clarity of each scene.

4

Making a Scene

When you think about films you love, you probably think
about specific scenes that stand out as unique and
memorable: the barnraising scenes in both *Witness* and *Seven
Brides for Seven Brothers;* the car-chase scene in *The French
Connection;* Charlie Chaplin holding onto the clock in *Modern
Times;* the boy drowning in quicksand in *Lawrence of
Arabia;* the boulder chasing Indiana Jones; the woodchipper
scene in *Fargo;* the scene of the Civil War wounded spread
out across acres of land in *Gone With the Wind;* and Elliott in
silhouette in *E.T.*, bicycling across the sky.

If you're a fan of horror, your list of memorable scenes
may include King Kong fighting the airplanes; the attack of
the killer tomatoes and the pod people; what Hannibal had
for dinner; and the Pillsbury Doughboy in *Ghost Busters*, who
dared to step on a church in New York City.

If you love comedy, you may recall the orgasm scene in
When Harry Met Sally; the unmasking of *Tootsie;* the piano-
hopping scene in *Big;* Kathy Bates ramming the little VW in
Fried Green Tomatoes; and Diane Keaton checking her baby
at the coat-check stand in *Baby Boom.*

In each of these scenes, the writer struck gold. How did
s/he do it? Why are those scenes there? What function do
they serve? How did the writer figure out what scenes were
needed and what scenes weren't?

When writing each of these memorable scenes, a writer
understood the function of the scene. But a writer went beyond

mere functionality to create vibrant images and strong emotions and a clear theme.

Scenes are the building blocks of the script. They deliver multiple layers of information. A great scene advances the story, reveals character, explores the theme, and builds an image.

In three of my books—*Making a Good Script Great, The Art of Adaptation,* and *Making a Good Writer Great*—I discuss the turning-point scene and the climactic scene. In this chapter I will discuss other types of scenes—some of which are used in every script and some of which are rarely used.

THE ESTABLISHING SCENE

Establishing scenes are designed to give context for the characters and the story and to start the story moving. Almost every film begins with an establishing scene. It sets a film's location. It answers the question: Where are we? Writer-director Devorah Cutler describes establishing or preparation scenes as setting "Tone, Town, and Time"—the style of a film, the place of a film, and the period of a film. I would add the word "Theme" to her list.

Watch the beginning of films to see how their context is established. If you watch the beginning of *Wall Street,* within the first minute or two, you will know the world of business and finance: the buildings, the morning rush, the energy of those in pursuit of money. The opening image begins to set up the theme of greed.

The opening scene of *Dead Poets Society* also uses images to establish its theme of overcoming conformity. The film begins as a school readies for its opening-day procession. Images depicting the school's tradition clearly set it up as a school with a long history of doing everything in a conventional way. Banners announce its educational and moral pillars of learning: Tradition. Honor. Discipline. Excellence. The principal gives his annual welcome speech. Finally, we're introduced to Keating, the person who brings creativity into this conformist culture.

In most scripts, the establishing scenes show a story's cultural world through wide-angle shots that may establish a school, a city, a country, a mansion, a corporation, a ballroom, a swamp, a plantation, a hospital, a football field.

A film's world may also be established with a closeup. *Schindler's List* opens on a closeup of a drawer. We see a man putting on elegant cuff links. He's preparing to go to a party to ingratiate himself to the Nazis. *Tootsie* opens with a closeup of an actor's makeup box.

Throughout a script, there can be many establishing shots. A car drives up to the door of a twenty-story corporate building—establishing a corporate world. A wide-angle shot of bucking broncs and Brahma bulls establishes the world of the rodeo.

Whether you choose a wide-angle shot or a closeup, the most important shot in your establishing scene is the first image. This image helps settle the audience and usher it into the movie-dream state. A filmmaker loses a great opportunity to get the story rolling immediately if this shot does not clearly orient us to the context of a film's context.

Remember the opening of *Cinema Paradiso?* Probably not. The opening shot shows a plant on a balcony overlooking the sea. What does it tell us? Nothing. The shot then widens to show an old lady talking on the phone to someone we don't know, who has been awakened by her phone call in the middle of the night. Who is he? Who is she? Since he's still in bed, and it's morning in Italy, then where is he? Now we have to do some rough time-zone calculations in our mind. If it's morning in Italy, and it's night where he is, does that mean he's in New York or Los Angeles or somewhere else? And what are they talking about? Who are they talking about? The film takes five minutes to find its focus, because its beginning has given us only confusion.

What might you have written for the opening scene? About ten minutes into this film, it becomes clear what needs to be established: A director gets news from his mother that one of the most important people in his life has just died. There are so many possibilities for a strong establishing scene. Certainly establishing the adult Toto on a set would have given us far more important information.

Another confusing beginning occurs in *Il Postino*. It's a charming, acclaimed, successful film that begins with a shot of a man on a bed, reading a postcard that we can't see clearly. We might wonder if this is a film about a sick man, since he's dressed but still in bed. We wonder if it's a film about a man who wants to travel to the place shown on the postcard. Then we see fishing boats, so we might wonder if it's a film about fishing. Although the fishing establishes something about the local community, it isn't an image that's connected with the main character.

We can see similar unclear beginnings in thousands of films. The film *In the Bedroom* begins with a number of images—including a community in the eastern part of the United States and a factory. But these images are never clearly linked to the main characters. Do the parents of the murderer own the factory? We never see the parents or Richard with his parents or the importance of the factory to the town, so why was the factory used as an important part of the film's setup?

Although most of these films become focused soon after their initial establishing shots, they each lost the critical opportunity to grab us at the outset by clearly setting up the world that we were about to enter.

You may want to watch the beginnings of these films as well as the beginnings of other Academy Award-nominated films to see which opening images clearly set up tone, town, time, and theme, and which don't.

THE EXPOSITION SCENE

The exposition scene is similar to the establishing scene. But whereas the establishing scene establishes the context of a film's world, the exposition scene gives the audience character and story information that it needs to know to understand the film. Exposition scenes can be the most difficult scenes to write, because a writer has to separate truly important and useful information from chat and ramblings. A writer also has to give us that important information in a way that is compelling and interesting.

Many writers give too much expositional information. In fact, dialogue usually isn't necessary for good exposition. Writer Jay Presson Allen recounts Alfred Hitchcock teaching her how few scenes she needed to communicate important information if she had the right image:

> When Hitch hired me for *Marnie,* I had never even read a screenplay. My approach to narrative was totally linear, so when it came to getting Sean [Connery] and Tippi [Hedren] from the altar to the reception to the honeymoon cabin on the ocean liner, I wrote three plodding scenes. Hitch gently suggested that we might pick up the pace by doing all this in one scene, i.e.,
>
> CLOSE UP. A large vase of roses with attached card saying: Congratulations!

A good exposition scene answers the question "Why?" before the audience has a chance to ask.

In the beginning of *Silence of the Lambs*, we learn why Crawford, the supervisor, decides to hire Clarice for a specific assignment:

                    CRAWFORD
          You're doing well. Top quarter of
          your class ... double major, psy-
          chology and criminality.

It's fast. Clear. Simple.

New writers often write exposition scenes that cover any number of unrelated matters: Where characters were born, what they're studying in school, what teachers they like, who their parents are, what kind of cars they want to drive, what are their favorite foods, what are their favorite colors, their shoe size, their favorite animal, their family trees, what kind of allergies they have. I call this kind of exposition "first-date dialogue"—chat, chat, chat. It's the getting-to-know-you scene that often does little to truly reveal character or advance the story. It's as if a writer was filling out a character's c.v., telling the audience all sorts of information they absolutely don't need to know. Although this backstory information can be helpful to a writer when creating characters, this sort of expository information should be cut unless it's essential to the story.

Sometimes, of course, this seemingly inconsequential information is germane to the story. If you're writing a story about the hardships of medical school, then what the character studies may be meaningful. If a film is about street racing, then the type of car the main character drives would be relevant.

THE CATALYST SCENE

A catalyst scene sets a storyline in motion. Within the first ten or fifteen minutes of a film, a catylist is necessary to start the story and propel it forward. Successful catalyst scenes that set up a story include:

The death of the gladiator's wife in *Gladiator,* quitting the job in *American Beauty,* the shooting in *The Sixth Sense,* the landing at Normandy in *Saving Private Ryan*, solving the math problem in *Good Will Hunting.*

The strongest catalyst scenes depict events and actions, rather than presenting discussions or verbal information. Although they're essential in the first fifteen minutes of a film, they can occur throughout the script. Two people meet at the first turning point and, as a result of the meeting, fall in love. Perhaps in Act Two the detective gets a fifth clue, which leads him to take a different approach to his investigation Perhaps at the second turning point, a protagonist learns about a new experimental drug that will cure her. These are catalysts that imply subsequent actions and, therefore, move a story forward.

THE LOVE SCENE

The love scene *defines* a love relationship. It also develops and proves that the couple is truly in love. Some writers presume that two characters will fall in love if he's defined as handsome and she's defined as beautiful. Obviously, more is needed than that.

A love scene might clarify any or all of the following: What do the lovers have in common? What is the magnetism that pulls them together? What threatens to pull them apart? What do they have to learn from each other?

In real life, our love shows through humor, through physical and verbal endearments, and through the sweet names lovers may call each other. We show love through the care we take of each other and through our intrinsic and learned understanding of each other's strengths and weaknesses. The chemistry between people may take many forms: passion, tenderness, sweetness, understanding, or shared intellectual curiosity.

Love scenes are usually subplot scenes, except in those few cases where the love relationship is the major plotline, as in *When Harry Met Sally* and *Sleepless in Seattle*.

Love scenes can take many forms.

The meeting scene: when Will gets Skylar's phone number in *Good Will Hunting*. The erotic scene: In *Dangerous Liaisons*, Valmont writes a love letter to one woman on the naked back of another. In *The Piano*, as Baines dusts the piano, it's clear that it's not the piano he's yearning to touch.

These scenes can be as tender and courageous as Guido taking Dora away on the green horse in *Life Is Beautiful*. They can be as subtle as the dance in the barn in *Witness* when John decides *not* to kiss Rachel. And they can be the climactic resolution that shows the lovers finally getting together, such as the end of *Sleepless in Seattle*.

THE CONFRONTATION SCENE

In a confrontation scene, one character confronts another character. This type of scene is often used as a means to allow a buried truth to surface. Everything that's been boiling up beneath the surface rises to the top, and problems that a character couldn't or wouldn't articulate are expressed. In a confrontation scene, subtext becomes text. There is no more hiding, and there's no room for misinterpretation. A character simply tells it like it is.

In *American Beauty*, Lester Burnham confronts the inauthenticity of his life. He wants more—more meaning from a job, more sexual and sensual fulfillment, something less shallow from his wife, and something richer and truer and deeper from life.

In one of the confrontation scenes in *American Beauty*, Lester confronts Carolyn about her mixed-up value system, which places her work and the sofa above what Lester sees as more important things in life.

                    LESTER
          Carolyn, when did you become so
          joyless? . . . This isn't life.
          It's just stuff. And it's become
          more important to you than living.
          Well, honey, that's just nuts.

A confrontation scene, in most cases, is about one character's anger directed specifically at the wrongs, real or imagined, done by another person or persons. Sometimes it's a moment that has been set up and, therefore, anticipated. At other times, it comes out of the blue, but makes sense because the audience has felt the character's hidden tensions.

In *Tootsie*, Michael confronts his agent, who didn't send him to the try-out for a play. The agent also confronts Michael about Michael's problems. This scene provided an opportunity for the writer to expose Michael's problem: He's difficult. He needs therapy.

THE PAY-OFF SCENE

A pay-off scene is an emotional, physical, and/or spiritual showdown. It's similar to a confrontation scene, but bigger in scope. It's the scene that the audience has been waiting for throughout a film.

If the sheriff in *High Noon* is waiting for the shoot-out, then a writer has to show the shoot-out. If Rocky is training for the fight, then a writer is obligated to show the fight. If the gladiator has set out to avenge the death of his family, then the pay-off scene is the avenging fight, when he finally kills the evil emperor. If Erin Brockovich is going to help bring the polluters to justice, then we have to see that scene. The guys in *The Full Monty* have to take it all off. A writer is obliged to pay off what has been set up. A promise has been made to the audience. If we don't see the pay-off scene, we'll feel cheated.

Sometimes a writer leaves out the pay-off scene because it might seem too obvious. Sometimes a writer presumes that we'll understand everything simply by seeing the result of the pay-off, rather than the pay-off itself. Although it's rare for an Academy Award-nominated film to leave out the pay-off, it has been done.

In *Il Postino*, Mario wants to marry Beatrice. One night, Beatrice comes to him. It's presumed that they sleep together. Meanwhile, Beatrice's aunt paces through the village with a rifle, looking for her niece, greatly upset by this developing romance. Then CUT TO the wedding. Suddenly we've been yanked from a scene of developing conflict to a happily-ever-after scene. What happened? Presumably there was an off-screen scene that resolved the aunt's anger and included Mario's and Beatrice's decison to get married. But, we didn't see it. Did we need the pay-off? The answer to that question seems to depend on your nationality. When I've discussed this film with my classes in Rome, Italians explained to me that the off-screen scene is obvious: In 1950s Italy, anytime a woman slept with a man, a wedding would immediately follow.

In terms of a broad international market, this scene may be less obvious, so I would consider it essential to pay off the conflict that built throughout Act Two and to pay off the development of the relationship.

In *Places in the Heart*, Edna works long and hard to plant cotton, and to be the first person to get the cotton to market in order to get an extra $100. We are waiting for that moment when she receives the check. We never see the check given to her, although later we know she received it. I would consider this a pay-off scene that was necessary to complete the story.

You might want to re-watch *Places in the Heart* and *Il Postino*. Did you expect them to offer pay-off scenes? Did you feel that pay-off scenes were set up? Did you feel you needed the clarity of pay-off scenes? Did you feel these scenes were obligatory?

A film's pay-off is usually its climax or sometimes its second turning point. The pay-off scene in *Il Postino* would have been placed at the second turning point. In *Places in the Heart*, it would have been the climactic scene. However, a pay-off scene can be set almost anywhere in a film if it is simply paying off something that was foreshadowed. If we see a closeup of a knife, the pay-off scene will show the knife being used, whether we're viewing the first murder at the end of the setup or at a first turning point or some murder during Act Two or Act Three.

THE RESOLUTION SCENE

A resolution scene shows the end or aftermath of a conflict that's been building throughout a story. Usually, these scenes are toward the end of a film. A resolution scene is the scene after the bad guy is captured or the mystery is solved or the bad feelings between two people are worked out. It's a scene that shows a return to a normal, more peaceful state. The point of the story has been made, characters have grown, and it's time to tie up loose ends. It's time for the audience to go home.

The resolution scene in *O Brother, Where Art Thou?* shows Ulysses Everett McGill out of jail and back with his wife. The resolution scene in *Sense and Sensibility* shows the right lovers are finally together and happily married. In the resolution scene in *Apollo 13*, the astronauts are safely back from their journey to the moon.

A resolution scene may also show a reconciliation between two people. Rather than simply solving a story problem, it also solves a relational problem. In *The Full Monty*, Gazz makes up with his ex-wife and finds renewed understanding. In *Magnolia*, the conflict between father and son is resolved. In *Jerry Maguire*, Jerry and Dorothy reconcile and are together again.

THE REALIZATION SCENE

A realization scene shows the moment when a character and/or the audience gets it. It's the "ah-ha." The Eureka moment. The moment of figuring it out. It's usually a moment of truth-telling or truth-showing. Sometimes it's the scene that shows a detective figuring out a mystery.

It might be the moment in *L.A. Confidential* when Jack figures out that Dudley is behind everything. Unfortunately, Jack found out too late. In *The Color Purple,* the realization scene occurs when Shug figures out that Celie is ready to kill Mister, so she runs to stop her. *The Sixth Sense*'s realization scene shows the moment when the character and the audience understand that Dr. Malcolm Crowe is dead. *The Green Mile*'s realization scene shows the moment when Paul realizes that John has magical, God-given powers to heal. *The Fugitive*'s realization scene shows Richard Kimble figuring out that Charlie Nichols is behind everything.

Toward the end of *Sense and Sensibility*, Elinor *realizes* that Edward Ferrars, the man she loves, never married Lucy, as Elinor had believed. At the beginning of the scene, Elinor and her family try to be polite by inquiring about Lucy, who they believe is now Mrs. Edward Ferrars.

> MARIAN
> I hope you have left Mrs. Ferrars
> well.

> MRS. DASHWOOD
> Is Mrs. Ferrars at the new parish?

Edward looks extremely confused.

> EDWARD
> No — my mother is in town.

> MRS. DASHWOOD
> I meant to enquire after Mrs.
> Edward Ferrars.

> EDWARD
> Then you have not heard - the news
> - I think you mean my brother - you
> mean Mrs. Robert Ferrars.

And he goes on to explain how Miss Steele transferred her affections from him to his brother, Robert.

> ELINOR
> Then you - are not married?

> EDWARD
> No.

Elinor bursts into tears as she *realizes* her dear Edward is still single and available.

Sometimes the moment of realization in a realization scene is not immediately evident, so neither the audience nor the character has an "ah-ha" experience. *Memento* downplayed this moment. It was almost there, and for a second, I almost got it. Then, it was gone. I felt the film needed a scene in which we suddenly understand the truth that we had been waiting the entire film to find. This was a hotly debated issue—to tell or not to tell? Some felt that not telling fit the style of the story. After all, the main character had a memory problem, so one might presume that he wasn't able to learn the truth. However, his problem was not in the logical function of his mind, it was in his memory, and those two mental functions are quite different. He was capable of learning the truth, he just wasn't capable of remembering it. I saw no reason why the audience couldn't know more than he did. In fact, part of the point of the film seemed to be to show his bad decisions, which showed how susceptible he was to manipulation as a result of his inability to remember.

In *Mulholland Drive*, the audience *needed* an "ah-ha" moment. Although Betty/Diane may not have been able to reach her own moment of truth (although a case could be made that the film may have worked better if she had been shown having a moment of realization right before killing herself), one only had to talk to audience members and read some reviews to realize that few understood the film because it didn't contain a realization scene.

THE DECISION SCENE

A realization scene is often followed by a decision scene, which shows a character deciding to act as a result of realization. If realization moves directly to action without showing a decision, the action scene can feel short-circuited, as if an arc has not been followed through. In *Stand by Me*, Vern tells the boys about the dead body and they *decide* they'll go to see it. In *The Castaway*, Chuck Noland finds the plastic door and *decides* to use it. In *The English Patient*, the nurse *decides* to stay behind and care for the English patient.

Usually a decision scene shows a character noticing, looking, observing, investigating, checking things out. Usually, it's followed immediately by an action scene that confirms that a decision has been made.

THE ACTION SCENE

Action scenes move a story forward. In an action scene, which usually follows a decision scene, characters do something—climb a mountain, chase a convict, come home to care for a parent, go to the doctor. In *The Fugitive's* action scenes, Kimble rents an apartment, searches through the computer, makes phone calls, finds his friend and asks for money, follows leads, and searches the one-armed man's apartment.

Even in non-action-oriented films, characters need to be *doing* something rather than just talking about something. In a character-driven film such as *You Can Count on Me*, action scenes show Samantha allowing her brother to stay with her, having an affair, and trying to resolve family issues.

THE REACTION SCENE

A reaction scene shows the reaction of one character to the action of another. In a *Die Hard* film, when the bad guys make a move, John McClane makes a counter move. In James Bond films, the villain starts the problem, and Bond reacts.

A reaction scene can focus on an emotional reaction, rather than a physical reaction. In *The Color Purple*, when Celie is snubbed during the party scene, she shows her emotional reaction by sticking out her tongue. In *Working Girl*, while Tess is working out on her bike, she discovers that her boss has stolen her idea. The scene focuses on her emotional reaction. She stops pedaling, devastated by this betrayal.

THE REALIZATION-DECISION-ACTION SCENE

Sometimes realization, decision, and action occur in the same scene. In *Witness*, when John Book has escaped up the ladder on the side of the silo, he hears Fergie coming closer to the bottom of the silo. John expects to be killed at any moment.

When he's not killed, he *realizes* he has a second chance, he sees a lever and *realizes* that there's corn up there, so he makes a *decision* to release the lever, and then *acts* by releasing the corn, which falls on Fergie, killing him. In this case, realization-decision-action are all in the same scene.

Often, these scenes form a scene sequence that shows realization, decision, action, and resolution scenes in a continuous stream. Playing out the sequence gives a character more dimension and the story more forward movement. In *Ghost,* Sam *realizes* that Molly is in danger and *decides* he has to do something about it. In the next scene, he *acts* by running to try to save her. His emotional *reaction* of concern for Molly leads him to new *action*—trying to get help from a psychic. This leads to new decisions, new actions, new reactions. Here the moment of realization and the moment of decision are part of the same scene. The action scene and reaction scene are separate scenes.

In *Big,* a scene sequence begins when Josh *decides* to give money to the vending machine, asking to be "big." In the next scene, he *realizes* he's big. This leads him to an emotional *reaction* scene as he realizes all the ramifications that "big" entails. And that leads him to a scene with new *action,* working for a toy company, trying to act as a big person even though his child-like behavior continues to manifest itself.

THE FLASHBACK SCENE

A flashback scene shows a past event. Usually seen through the point of view of the main character, the flashback is usually used to reveal a past traumatic event that has not yet been resolved or to unravel a mystery from the past.

The flashbacks in *Ordinary People* help us understand that Conrad doesn't want to face the truth. In this film, flashbacks are used for psychological effect, since the past needs to be unraveled in order to find healing in the present. Sometimes a flashback shows us a lie. In *The Usual Suspects*, Verbal's story, presented as a flashback, is assumed to be the truth, but at a film's end, we realize it's all been made up. Flashback scenes are often found at the end of films based on Agatha Christie's detective stories, when the detective recounts "who done it" and the story flashes back to show how it was done.

New writers love flashback scenes, which they often use to provide backstory information that's not essential to the story. Such a scene might show an abusive childhood or introduce parents or show other sorts of childhood experiences.

Sometimes, when I try to talk writers out of unnecessary flashbacks, they tell me that these scenes reveal character. True, they do reveal character, but they're not revealing the particular aspects of the character that we need to know. Since a flashback puts the emphasis on the past, a flashback can sacrifice the more important present life of the character. Many times, a line or two of dialogue in the present can tell us everything we need to know about the past, without flashing back to some scene that can stop the flow of a film.

Some writers love flashbacks because they seem "cinematic," although they often stop a story's flow. And some writers love them because they can further "layer" their characters, although those layers might sacrifice the development of the character in the present.

THE FRAME

The most overused type of flashback scene is the frame. A frame is actually two scenes that bookend a film. A character begins the story by telling the audience that he or she is going to tell us a story. Then the story flashes back and tells the story, and, at the end, we return to the present, where the character now informs us that the story has ended. The highly unsuccessful film *Hudson Hawk* used this obvious technique. So did the classic *Citizen Kane*, although this was not such an overused technique in the 1940s.

We can see the frame in *The Mission,* which begins with someone talking. We don't know who it is, and we don't know what he's talking about. This opening frame actually gets in the way of the more powerful scene that follows: a priest being tied to a cross and sent to his death as that cross is tossed into a raging river.

The Green Mile also uses a frame. Paul, as an old man, looks back at the days when he met John Coffey. The story then flashes back to the events in the past and, at the end, returns for some final words from Paul. *Saving Private Ryan* begins with a frame and then flashes back to the incident of trying to save Private Ryan.

I find these particular three frames clunky and awkward and unnecessary. In *The Green Mile,* the frame itself was unclear. Where were these people? Although we're told that they were at a nursing home, they had far too much freedom, and at least some of them were far too healthy to be in a nursing home. The information that Paul is 108 years old, which comes out in the ending frame scene, seems merely interesting, but not pertinent. We already know about John. We already know about Paul. Talking about them at the end doesn't give us more necessary information.

The frame in *Saving Private Ryan* also seemed unnecessary. Although emotional, the point is well made within the body of the work. For some reason, Steven Spielberg seems to love frames. He used similar frames in both *Schindler's List* and *Saving Private Ryan,* both of which seemed to cloud the focus of their stories. (I believe that these frames were his idea, since they function in much the same way in both films.) You may want to re-watch these two films to consider how you feel about their frames.

On the other hand, *Amadeus* and *Stand by Me* use frames that create an essential resonance between the past and the present. *Stand by Me* is a film about friendship and about fathers and sons. The frame helps these ideas resonate as Gordy looks back to his childhood friendships with Chris and Vern and Eddie and recognizes "I never had any friends later on like the ones I had when I was twelve. Jesus, does anyone?" This flashback also shows the connection between Gordy the grown-up, successful writer and Gordy the young storyteller.

In *Amadeus*, the frame reinforces a theme of mediocrity, showing that the talented and brilliant Mozart, even after his death, continued to be a thorn in the side of the mediocre but long-lived Salieri.

As a script consultant, I recommend using a frame only when a writer needs to set up a strong resonance between past and present. When trying to decide whether to cut a frame or flashback scene, I ask, "Is this relevant? Is this essential? What is gained by it? Can this information be conveyed in a more dramatic way?"

THE REVELATION SCENE

The Revelation Scene, the Epiphany Scene, and the Reflection Scene are three types of scenes that we rarely see in films, but are important if you're working with philosophical or spiritual subject matter.

In a revelation scene, a spiritual entity reveals itself to a character, sometimes through a physical presence, sometimes through dialogue. The effect of this revelation is powerful enough to motivate the character's actions throughout the story.

This spiritual entity is not just any otherworldly being. I'm not talking about a poltergeist or a ghost or the devil who provide a negative influence, forcing a character to retreat or overcome a destructive power in order to get back to a normal life. A revelation comes from a positive influence, from a spirit who moves the character away from a normal, ordinary life into a life that is extraordinary.

Revelation scenes are often used in religious films, such as *Song of Bernadette*, in which Bernadette sees a vision of the Virgin Mary, and the *Joan of Arc* films, in which Joan hears voices that tell her what to do. In the revelation scene in *Resurrection*, Edna realizes she has powers to heal. In the revelation scene in *Phenomenon*, George realizes that he has enhanced brainpower. In the revelation scene in *Field of Dreams*, Ray hears a voice telling him to build a baseball field. Each of these scenes acts as a catalyst for the character who is forced into a story that s/he never dreamed of entering before receiving the revelation. Each of these scenes change the direction of the character's life. These characters cannot be the same after the revelation. Their actions, their emotions, their attitudes toward life are all affected.

THE EPIPHANY SCENE

An Epiphany is defined as a spiritual or philosophical moment of awakening, a shift in consciousness, a moment of insight into the whole of things or into the meaning of things. Usually, an epiphany happens instantaneously, rather than a change of consciousness that may take place over a long period of time.

After experiencing an epiphany, we see life differently, and this may or may not affect our actions, but it always affects our emotional state and our value system and our attitudes.

We rarely see epiphany scenes in films, partly because they can be static and are essentially stand-alone scenes without any intrinsic connection to other scenes in a film. But sometimes these scenes have worked well. In *Stand by Me*, Gordy wakes early in the morning by his campsite. He sits on the railroad track and writes. Suddenly, a deer appears, stops, smells, and slowly moves away. In voice-over, the adult Gordy reflects on that moment:

```
              NARRATOR (V.O. )
     The freight woke up the other guys
     and it was on the tip of my tongue
     to tell them about the deer, but I
     ended up not doing it. That was one
     thing I kept to myself. I've never
```

> spoken or written of it until just
> now, today. But for me it was the
> best part of the trip. The cleanest
> part.

For Gordy, this moment gave another layer of meaning to the whole trip.

Did this moment change Gordy's life? No. It wasn't a revelation that pushed him into a new reality. But something changed inside of him. He found some meaning that he could turn to, whenever things went wrong. In Stephen King's book *Different Seasons*, from which *Stand by Me* was adapted, he mentions those times when he's remembered this moment—the first day in Vietnam, the death of his mother, the illness of his son. Each of these times became more bearable because he remembered his epiphany with the deer. Although a film can't expand on this moment in the same way that a book can, as you watch the film, you may feel a sense of the importance of this encounter.

In *A Room With a View*, George has an epiphany as a result of seeing a man killed in the plaza. Lucy tries to dismiss what she's seen so that it doesn't affect her, but George, who has been searching for the meaning of life, has an epiphany, proclaiming, "Something tremendous has happened!"

George finds meaning within this episode. It doesn't change his actions, but it does stop his brooding and it leaves him more open to the miracle of love that he experiences with Lucy.

THE REFLECTION SCENE

Related to the epiphany scene is the reflection scene—a scene in which a character moves away from action and reflects on what has happened. It's a scene that quiets down a film's action, allowing a character to take a breath and think about what's going on before moving back to action.

Some excellent reflection scenes are found in *Working Girl*. In one scene, Tess discovers her boyfriend in bed with another woman. She then walks to the river, where she reflects on the situation. In another scene, while on a ferry, she reflects on her situation. Reflection scenes are usually written very sparsely:

```
EXT. STATEN ISLAND FERRY — NIGHT
TESS STANDING at the bow, staring out.
```

Later, there's another reflection and reaction scene from Tess when she realizes her boss betrayed her:

```
Tess collapses on the couch, crying. She
picks up a photograph of KATHERINE. She
studies it, wiping away tears, pulling
herself together. She puts it back down,
determined.

After this moment of reflection,Tess moves
into action.
```

In *The Fugitive*, Deputy Sam Gerard reflects several times on the situation he's presented with. As we see him smoking a cigar and thinking, we can almost read his thoughts: "Where is he? Am I missing anything?" Later he looks at the handcuffs that once held Kimble and seems to wonder, "Where could he be?" Later, he looks at the picture of the crime scene and then looks out the window, clearly concerned that he's not been able to figure it out.

In *The Green Mile*, after every execution and after each difficult episode on Block E, Paul sits at home, listening to the radio, drinking a glass of wine, and just reflecting.

Reflection scenes are difficult to write and demand a highly skilled actor who can communicate thoughts without verbally stating them. Many writers don't write these scenes. Sometimes they're added to the script by the director. But I recommend that writers add them to their scripts when necessary, so that this reflective emotional layering is not forgotten.

I can't find any reflection scenes in the actual script of *The Fugitive*, even though they worked so well in a film to define another dimension of Sam Gerard's character. However, they're written in the script of *The Green Mile:*

> Paul enters in darkness, hangs his hat. He
> drifts into the kitchen, clicks on the ra-
> dio. SOFT MUSIC BEGINS: Gene Austin sing-
> ing "Did You Ever See a Dream Walking?"

> He pours a drink at the kitchen table,
> takes a sip, lays the glass down. Jan
> sleepily appears from the darkness behind
> him ... She can sense the weight on his
> soul. She comes to him, folds his head
> into her arms. They stand that way, he
> drawing strength and she giving it, as the
> music plays on ...

A later scene description gives us another feeling of Paul thinking, reflecting.

> Paul is wide awake, staring at the dark.

A similar scene uses the radio as a device that quiets this character and leads him to reflection.

> Paul is at the kitchen table in the wee
> hours, listening to the radio as usual,
> sipping beer.

When watching, we realize that a thought process is going on, and that the scene is not just about listening to the radio or drinking. Notice the feeling of darkness and quiet this scene achieves by showing actions that imply an emotional state.

SCENES OF MAGIC AND WONDER

Film can take us into another world. Sometimes this is a world of altered states and new realities that is shown through scenes depicting visions and dreams and fantasies. Such scenes swoop us up and let us soar into other worlds. Superman takes Lois Lane on a magical flight. In *The Wizard of Oz*, Dorothy is swept up, magically, by a tornado.

In *Out of Africa*, the magical airplane scene takes us into the beauty of Africa. For Karen Blixen (and for us moviegoers), it was one of the most magical moments in her whole time in Africa. *The English Patient* has its magical fresco scene, as Kip shows Hana the frescoes in the bombed-out church. He fastens a rope around her waist and then swings her through the air, from one fresco to another.

Magic-and-wonder scenes aren't just about flying or soaring. In *Mary Poppins*, Julie Andrews and Dick Van Dyke step into a painting on the sidewalk and enter a new reality. In *The Purple Rose of Cairo*, the movie star steps out of the picture and into the audience.

Many magical scenes are part of a three-act scene sequence that has a beginning, middle, and end, and turning points to help define its structure. These scenes work best when there is some feeling of structure, rather than just focusing on the wondrous act itself. If you watch the flying scene in the first *Superman* film, you can feel the three-act structure. In Act One, Superman comes to Lois, and she takes his hand. At the first turning point, they start to soar. During Act Two, she feels the wonder of the experience. At the second turning point she lets go and starts to fall. He catches her, and in Act Three they finish the flight. In the Resolution, they land, back on earth.

When watching *The English Patient* fresco scene, I always feel that there's a beat missing, which would have been the second turning point of the scene. We could define the structure of this fresco scene as: Act One, Kip takes Hana to the church. At the first turning point, she is lifted up into the air. During Act Two of the scene, she soars through the air in wonder at the fresco's beauty. Then, suddenly, we're at the climax: She's down on the ground, kissing Kip. This could have been structured with a second turning point, which might have been a moment when she looks at Kip and makes the connection that the man who has given her this joy is the man that she loves. This moment could have moved from her connection with the frescoes to a realization of her connection with Kip before coming down to kiss him. Watch the scene and see if you feel this missing beat.

Sometimes a magic-and-wonder scene is implied in a script, but it's never played out. As a result, the audience can feel disappointed, frustrated, or simply blasé about the scene. *Pearl Harbor* has a missed opportunity for a magic-and-wonder scene. The night before Pearl Harbor was bombed, Danny asks Evelyn if she's ever seen Pearl Harbor at sunset. "Yes," she says. "But from the air?" he asks. At that moment, I expected to see a memorable, magical scene: Pearl Harbor at sunset, the night before the battle. But we never got it. We saw a scene of two people in a cockpit kissing.

I expected similar magic years ago when the much-talked-about *Hook* was released. Ah, flying through the air with Peter Pan. No. All of its magical scenes were truncated rather than built up.

When writing a magic-and-wonder scene, capture the mood of the experience through the words that you choose, and try to give the scene a definite structure. This might mean showing the preparation for the scene, adding turning points, and then giving it a solid ending so it doesn't just peter out.

THE SHOW-STOPPER SCENE

A show-stopper scene is a big production number, much like the scenes that we often see at the act break in a musical play. These scenes sometimes break open a play or film, anchoring it in some charming way that provides vibrant style and energy, often creating the scene we remember the best. In *Big*, the show-stopper scene is the piano scene, when Josh and his new boss play chopsticks with their feet. In *Billy Elliot*, it's the midpoint scene when Billy and his teacher dance together, flying across the screen. In *Beauty and the Beast* it's the "Be Our Guest" song, when all the utensils dance as they welcome Belle to the table.

Although a show-stopper doesn't intrinsically need to be around a film's midpoint, in each of these cases, that's where it's located. It's almost exactly where it would appear in a two-act play—right at the first-act curtain.

Each of these examples revolves around music—playing and/or singing and/or dancing. However, a show-stopper scene wouldn't need to be in a musical. I could imagine creating a circus scene or a chase scene or a sports scene that could work as a show-stopper. A case could be made that the training montage in *Rocky* is a show-stopper, defined partly by its background music and partly by its development of the action to a crescendo. For a show-stopper scene to work, it needs to be a culmination of a character arc that shows that something has been achieved, the character has moved, and at least a partial transformation has been gained.

Show-stopper scenes build by becoming bigger and bigger as the scene progresses. What begins as a single "Chop Sticks" solo in *Big* expands to a duet with more and more movement and energy. The music and dancing become faster and faster. What begins as a simple dinner scene in *Beauty and the Beast* builds with the addition of more characters, more dancing, more singing, more color, more energy. When creating a show-stopped scene, think of the word "MORE." Keep building the scene, and don't be afraid to be outrageous.

THE MONTAGE

A montage is not a single scene but a series of brief scenes and/or often single shots, usually without dialogue, and usually designed to show the passing of time, quickly moving a story forward. A montage implies development, often in a relationship, although it doesn't show all the steps of development, since its scenes are too short. We, in the audience, fill in the blanks.

One of the most overused montage sequences is the falling-in-love montage. I've seen thousands of them in my work as a script consultant, and they all look the same. Such a tired sequence might be:

a) Champagne with dinner at an elegant restaurant; two lovers gaze into each other's eyes.

b) Walking on the beach at sunset holding hands.

c) Rolling around in water and sand.

d) Split screen: He's thinking of her. She's thinking of him.

e) Their first kiss.

f) Autumn leaves turn to gold as calendar pages fly off the calendar, showing the passage of time.

The best falling-in-love montages are much more original than this, giving us information about the nature of a particular love, and implying the transformations that occur when two people find each other.

A great montage not only moves a story forward, but it also has its own emotional component, which usually deepens the audience's understanding and empathy with the characters. Often, the montage doesn't just move forward in time, but shows that a character is moving toward a transformation.

One of my favorite falling-in-love montages comes from *Tootsie*. It begins at the farm, when Dorothy/Michael is given the child, Amy, to hold. Michael is not fond of children, and he hardly knows what to do with Amy. For a moment, he holds her at arms' length, but then brings her close. A song plays over the montage, further setting the mood and reinforcing Dorothy/Michael's feelings. Short scenes show Dorothy making dinner with Julie, Julie giving Dorothy some frosting to lick from her finger, eating dinner while Dorothy watches Julie in the light, and finally all singing around the piano.

It's clear what's happening in this montage. Michael is transforming as a result of his love of Julie. As you watch it, you'll probably note that it is reflective rather than active. We see Dorothy/Michael observing, feeling, responding. The transformation that Michael goes through during the course of the montage allows him to truly see Julie as more than just an object. He sees her as a human being. During the montage, Michael becomes a more dimensional person, worthy of Julie's love.

Both *Ghost Busters* and *Tootsie* have "becoming success-ful" montages. *Ghost Busters* has its montage at the beginning of Act Two. It shows that the unsuccessful ghost busters have become successful and are now on the cover of every magazine and appearing on every talk show. At the midpoint of *Tootsie*, a montage shows Dorothy on a series of magazine covers, establishing her popularity. She's achieved success.

Secrets & Lies has several montages that show Maurice at work, taking photographs of weddings, dogs, children, and a woman who has been scarred by an accident. In *Big*, Josh misses his boyhood. A montage shows us the kids in his class having their class photo taken, boys playing ball, boys in a convertible, and ends with Josh's line, "I want to go home."

Sometimes a montage presents necessary but potentially boring information quickly. A montage may show a student researching in a library and end a few seconds later with the student completing a paper. It might show a detective interviewing a series of people who don't have any new information to give him but establishes how thorough this detective's investigation is. A montage might show the tedious preparation for a trial, as in the film *A Few Good Men*.

Although most montages don't contain dialogue within the body of the montage, a few do. *A Few Good Men*'s preparation-for-court montage uses dialogue as well as visuals to take us through the strategy of Kaffee, Jo, and Sam as they prepare their case.

```
54. INT. THE APARTMENT - NIGHT

   A SERIES OF LAP DISSOLVES showing Kaffee's
   apartment getting messier and messier with
   papers, cartons, books, and pizza boxes.

   A) Flipping through documents and refer-
   ence books.

   B) Jo writing something on the blackboard.
```

C) Sam on the witness stand again.

D) Kaffee paying for another pizza.

E) Sam dozing.

Over all of the above we hear:

                KAFFEE (V.O.)
Now they drew the court members
this afternoon. Seven men, two
women, five Navy, four Marines. All
officers with line experience. Neither of the women have children. So
that's a bad break, but remember,
poker faces. Don't flinch in front
of the court members. Something
doesn't go our way, don't hang your
head, don't shift in your seat,
don't scribble furiously. Whatever
happens, you have to look like it's
exactly what you <u>knew</u> was gonna
happen.

The clock reads 1:37 and KAFFEE, in
sweatpants, is pacing around slowly with
his baseball bat. SAM and JO are listening
to a lecture for the 14th time.

                KAFFEE
When you pass me documents -

                JO/SAM
        (by rote, Sam waking up)
Do it swiftly, but don't look over-
anxious.

                KAFFEE
              (beat)
And don't wear that perfume in
court, it wrecks my concentration.

                    JO
      Really?

                  KAFFEE
      I was talking to Sam.

Obviously the varied types of scenes covered in this chapter are not the only types of scenes that you can create for a film. In other chapters, I'll be discuss thematic scenes, transformational themes, scenes involving twists and turns.

Knowing the function of a scene can help you figure out where to put its focus, how to set its tone, and to figure out how the scene should advance the action. It can help you determine which scenes you need for your particular script and where to place the scene. And then the real work begins—how to write it so that it's dramatic, unique, and memorable.

5

Twists and Turns, Secrets and Lies

A writer is a revealer. The clever writer knows what to reveal, how to reveal it, and when to reveal it. The clever writer juggles truth and lies, misinterpretations, and miscommunications. The clever writer works with surprises, twisting and turning a story, keeping the audience in a state of anticipation, anxiously waiting to see what will happen next. How does a writer construct plausible yet surprising twists and turns?

Almost every great script has turns in its story. A turn takes a story in a new direction, provides variety, begins new developments, and changes a story's focus. At the minimum, a well-structured three-act script will have two turning points: one that turns the story from Act One into Act Two and one that turns the story from Act Two to Act Three. The script might also have a turn at its midpoint.

Most scripts will have more than just two or three turns. Some additional turns will come from subplot turning points, which will usually have two turning points and sometimes a midpoint turn. Smaller subplots might have only one turn.

The fewer turns in a script, the more space it has to develop relationships and conflicts. The more turns in a script, the more the story will zigzag with new developments, twists, and surprises. However, you need to be concerned if you're turning the story in new directions every few pages, since too many turns don't allow you time to develop your characters and story.

DEFINING THE TURN

What is a turning point? In my book *Making a Good Script Great*, I ascribe the following six attributes to a turning point. It is an event that:

- turns the action in a new direction,
- takes us into a new arena and gives us a sense of a different focus for the action,
- declares a decision or commitment on the part of the main character,
- raises the story's central question again, and makes us wonder about its answer,
- raises the stakes,
- pushes the story into the next act.

In most cases, the writer prepares the audience for the upcoming turn. Just as you look ahead when driving and see a bend in the road, you can also see a turn coming in a story. You may not know what's around the curve, but you know you're going into the curve and you expect something new to present itself.

A turning point is not a surprise, although its execution may be. Usually, scene sequences lead up to it. One of my favorite turning-point scenes is in *Dead Poets Society* when the boys leave for the cave to start the Dead Poets Society. This turn is not a surprise. Preceeding this turn is a series of scenes that sets up the turn: The boys discover Keating's picture in an old yearbook and see that he was part of the Dead Poets Society. They show the yearbook to Keating and ask him about it. He mentions the cave where the society used to meet. The boys come together and discuss going there that night. Todd doesn't want to go, but the other boys convince him to come with them. They leave.

It's a beautifully constructed first-turning-point scene that prepares us for Act Two's development, which shows what happens when conformist boys from a conformist culture let their creative juices loose.

In almost every Academy Award-nominated film, the turning points are clear, and usually expressed through action:

Apollo 13: The first turning point is the blast-off for the moon. The midpoint is, "Houston, we have a problem." And at the second turning point, Ken figures out how to get them back to earth.

Braveheart: The first turning point is William Wallace's decision to fight the English. The second turning point occurs when Robert the Bruce wants to meet with William, but Bruce's father betrays them, leading to William's capture.

Beauty and the Beast: At the first turning point, Belle is captured and chooses to stay with the Beast in exchange for her father's freedom. During Act Two she falls in love with the Beast, and wants to stay with him of her own free will. However, she learns that her father is in danger, so she decides to leave. The Beast allows her to leave, even though it might mean he will never return to his normal state before the last rose petal falls. Her leaving is the second turning point, which leads to Gaston's decision to bring a mob to try to kill the beast.

When Harry Met Sally: At the first turning point, Harry and Sally start their friendship. At the second turning point, they sleep together.

Cinema Paradiso: At the first turning point, Alfredo makes a deal with Toto: If Toto gives him the answers to the test they're taking, Alfredo will allow Toto to work the projector. At the story's midpoint, a fire breaks out at the cinema. At the second turning point, Alfredo has died, and Toto is returning for the funeral.

Although most turning points are shown through action, sometimes a turning point uses dialogue to push the story forward.

Fargo: At the first turning point, Marge gets a phone call about a murder. She begins the case. At the second turning point the police hear that something strange is going on at the lake. This leads Marge to the lake, where she finds one of the bad guys and the body parts of another.

The Piano: At the first turning point, Baines agrees to save Ada's piano and discusses the proposition with Stewart. He then tells Ada the deal: He has saved her piano in exchange for lessons. The lessons lead to an affair between Ada and Baines. At the second turning point, Stewart finds out about Ada's affair with Baines, which leads to a confrontation and, eventually, to Baines and Ada leaving together at the climax.

Quiz Show: The evidence of wrongdoing in Act One leads to the decision to call a Grand Jury at the first turning point. At the second turning point Snodgrass can now prove that the show has been rigged.

Silence of the Lambs: At the first turning point, Hannibal Lecter asks Clarice, "Would you like me to help you find Buffalo Bill?" Immediately after that, another woman is kidnapped by Bill. We've been prepared for that turn all through Act One, as we've learned about Buffalo Bill and his kidnapping. This turn leads to Clarice's investigation in Act Two. At the second turning point, Clarice figures out who's the murderer. This information turns the story into Act Three, where she confronts the murderer, captures him, and rescues his next victim, despite great danger to herself.

Each turn takes the story in a new direction, and also opens up further explorations of theme and character and conflict. Turns are not arbitrary. They must integrate with all story elements, maintaining a story's inner logic, while providing surprises and a sense of organic movement from act to act.

Notice that each turning point mentioned above, whether an action or dialogue, *implies* the action that follows. Each turn has consequences that play out throughout the next act.

Notice that the turn usually brings about trouble, trouble, trouble. There's going to be conflict. Someone isn't going to like what's happening. There'll be complications, some of them unexpected: The boys in *Dead Poets Society* had no reason to expect that their harmless prank would end up in suicide. Michael had no reason to believe that his desire for a job and his acting ability would lead to the possibility of being sued, his inability to get the girl, a compromised friendship, an angry roommate, men falling in love with him, and a transformation of his character.

CREATING THE TWIST

The twist is different from the turn. The twist is an action that suddenly shows us that things are not what they seem to be. It's the moment when everything adds up—we learn the truth, but the truth isn't what we thought. It's a surprise. It's an "ah-ha." It isn't prepared for, but when it happens, it makes total sense. A great twist is visceral rather than intellectual. It hits us in the gut. When a twist occurs, it's not unusual to hear a yelp or a sigh or an intake of breath from the audience.

A twist will usually occur at a story's structural point, generally at its first or second turning point, the midpoint, or the climax. Twists are difficult to construct. They need to be set up so they make sense. Yet, their setups have to conceal information that would give the twist away too soon.

The Usual Suspects has a twist at its climax when we, and the interrogator, learn that we've been had. *The Sixth Sense* has a twist at its climax, when Malcolm realizes that he's dead. *L.A. Confidential* has a twist at its second turning point, when we realize that the captain of the police force is behind all the crime. *Thelma & Louise* has a twist at its first turning point when, in a rage, Louise unexpectedly shoots and kills Harlan. *A Beautiful Mind* has a twist right after its midpoint, when we realize that John Nash is mentally ill. *The Crying Game* has a twist at its midpoint, when we learn that Dil is a man. *Witness* has a twist at its first turning point, when John Book realizes that Schaefer is behind the murder.

Notice that none of these twists occurs early in the story. The ones in *Witness* and *Thelma & Louise* don't occur until the very end of Act One. It may be possible to do an early Act-One twist, and someday someone will do one, but a surprise is a thwarting of expectations, which often takes a good

bit of time to establish so that they can be successfully re-
versed with a twist.

Notice that each of these twists reveals a hidden truth to
the audience and the protagonist.

Creating secrets

Twists almost always rely on secrets. When a writer deals
with secrets, five questions must be answered:

- Why is the secret in the story?
- Who has the secret?
- From whom is the secret kept?
- When is the secret revealed?
- To whom is the secret revealed?

The longer a secret is held, the more opportunity the writer
has to surprise us with a strong twist. In most scripts, the
protagonist and the audience discover the secret at the same
time, often by the second turning point. This gives a writer
the opportunity to play out the consequences of learning the
secret in Act Three.

What makes a great twist?

Two films contain almost the exact same twist—*Witness* and
L.A. Confidential. Both have a moment when the protagonist
and the audience simultaneously understand that the head of
the police force is behind the crime.

Try to recall how your experiences of these two twists
differs. You were probably surprised by the twist in *Witness,*
but you probably did not feel like you had just been hit in
your gut. You probably had a much stronger visceral reaction
to the twist in *L.A. Confidential.* Why? What is the difference
between them? How can you use an understanding of these
two different twists to help you create a gut-wrenching twist
in your own screenplays?

In *Witness,* the twist comes toward the end of Act One,
leading into the first turning point. There has been very little
time to set up our expectations. We heard Schaefer's name

mentioned only once—during the crime scene investigation, when John Book says, "Where is Schaefer? Get him down here now." We meet Schaefer for the first time toward the end of Act One, when Book goes to his home to tell him that McFee is behind the crime. Schaefer then asks Book, "Who else knows about this?" And Book answers, "Just you and me."

Schaefer seems like a perfectly nice guy, but we haven't had enough time to form a strong impression of him. It's an early twist, so we have few expectations.

When Book figures out that Schaefer is behind the crime, the twist comes through dialogue, which is less dramatic than action. Book remembers his conversation with Schaefer: "Who else knows about this?" And Book remembers his response, "Just you and me." At that moment, Book and the audience realize that Schaefer is in on the crime and that Book's life is in danger, as are Rachel's and Samuel's lives. The power of this twist is somewhat dissipated because the dialogue comes as a voice-over rather than as a direct conversation between the two characters

A gut-wrenching twist wasn't necessary in *Witness* and may not have worked. A stronger twist may have affected the balance and structure of the story, since setting up expectations about Shaefer would have created a longer Act One. A stronger dramatic twist would have hardened the tone of a film, which was not intended to be as hard-edged as *L.A. Confidential*.

Look at the twist in *L.A. Confidential*. Dudley appears in a number of scenes in Act One and Act Two. He's introduced as the captain of the police within the first five minutes of the film. He seems amiable. He even gives out eggnog to his men. Who can dislike a guy who gives out Christmas cheer? We expect that he's a nice enough guy. And throughout the film, we hear Dudley spout off about integrity. He stands up for Bud when Bud won't snitch on his partner. Dudley wants to be effective. He wants a clean town. He says, "A heinous crime demands a swift resolution."

If Dudley had been set up as an impeccably nice guy for two acts, we may not have believed the twist when it happened. So the writers shaded in certain compromising qualities for the captain. To achieve this, Dudley makes frequent statements that tell us that he's willing to compromise to get the job done. He tells Exley, "You have the eye for human weakness, but not the stomach," which implies that Dudley has both the eye and the stomach for it. Dudley beats up criminals who want to move in on "his town." We see him as someone willing to make compromises to get things done. But we *never* expect him to be behind the murders.

The twists in both *Witness* and *L.A. Confidential* occur in unlikely settings. Both John Book and Jack Vincennes go to their bosses' homes to talk about what they discovered. We know that both John Book in *Witness* and Jack in *L.A. Confidential* have been to these homes before, implying casual and close relationships. In both films, the homes are warm and cozy, and the men do homey things. In *Witness*, Schaefer's daughter answers the door, and his wife greets Book. The scene makes us believe that they are best friends. In *L.A. Confidential*, Dudley is shown in his home wearing a bathrobe. He and Vincennes talk, he starts to make tea, but then he turns around from this simple activity and—wham—he shoots Jack. We, in the audience, add everything up, and the third act plays out the result of this sudden twist.

One of the best story twists occurs at the end of *The Usual Suspects*. It helped make *The Usual Suspects* one of the most talked-about films of 1995 and, no doubt, helped the film win the Academy Award for Best Original Screenplay.

The twist comes after we've heard the entire story of a team of criminals. We've been led to believe that Verbal, the poor, crippled narrator of this tale, is a follower. We think that he is manipulated by circumstances. But, in the film's final moments, we suddenly find that Verbal's manipulated his story for his own dark purposes.

This twist is subtly prepared for by showing Verbal's interrogation, during which we see him repeatedly glance at objects in the room before continuing his story. At the film's end, all of these glances suddenly add up, as Agent Dave figures out that Verbal used the objects around the room as the basis for his fabricated story. Then we, and Agent Dave, realize that Verbal is really the very powerful and sinister Keyser Soze.

Many times, a twist works because a character's moment of realization comes too late. If only he had known! But of course he couldn't, because a writer knew that if this character realized the truth too quickly, all the fun, suspense, conflict, tension, and cleverness would be lost.

The twists in both *L.A. Confidential* and *The Usual Suspects* happened too late to help the supporting characters. By the time Vincennes gets it in *L.A. Confidential*, he's already shot and dying. By the time Agent Dave gets it in *The Usual Suspects*, Keyser Soze has disappeared. In both cases, the audience gets it at the same moment the character gets it. If the audience doesn't get it, the twist doesn't work.

How to achieve the twist

A successful twist requires a very carefully constructed story that is driven by a character's intention.

Achieving a carefully constructed story may require the writer to outline or to write out the off-screen scenes. This technique can help writers keep track of what's happening behind the scenes and help them make decisions about which scenes need to be shown to the audience and which scenes need to be off-screen. Sometimes, twists that may seem clever and give us the "ah-ha" experience don't add up when we re-think them. We recall all the clues leading up to the twist and think, "If the ending is true, then the clues leading up to it don't make sense." This problem can be seen in a film like *No Way Out*. When the twist came at the very end, we learn who Lt. Commander Tom Farrell really is. But, when we trace the story back from this twist, we realize that the film simply doesn't make sense. If it doesn't add up, it doesn't work.

In a twist, we see the consequences of the antagonist's actions, but we don't see the antagonist at work. The antagonist's secret actions are off-screen. We keep wondering: "Who is behind all of this?" We either have no idea whatsoever until the twist occurs (as in *L.A. Confidential*) or we suspect someone else. (In *Witness* we know it's McFee but don't suspect that Schaefer is in on it.)

I don't believe you can ever achieve a twist with completely honest characters. Twists depend on corruption, dishonesty, distrust, and uncertainty. We presume that the antagonist is honest—until our presumption is proven wrong.

To create the twist, the audience must be respected. A writer must not make patsies or suckers of the audience. The twist must be logical. A writer must never set up the audience in a way that makes them feel stupid for not having figured out the twist. Nor must a writer throw in a twist that's arbitrary. The audience must be able to think back through all the clues and find that both clues and the twist make sense. This technique will also help you make sure you've worked out your plot backward and forward, so that everything on and off-screen leads to a believable twist. Determine where you want the twist to occur, and then make sure your foreshadowing subtly leads to it.

Potential twists that never happened

Sometimes writers miss an opportunity to create a twist. A twist may be built into a story but a writer doesn't play it out. In *Mulholland Drive*, we had an expectation about who Betty was and what the mystery was about. We were led to believe that Betty is a kind and talented new actress, trying to help solve the mystery of Rita's amnesia. Our expectation proved to be wrong at the second turning point of the film, when we hear knocking and then see a very down-trodden Betty, who we're told is really Diane. But instead of getting an "ah-ha" or "wow," many of us got a "Wait a moment!" or "Huh?" or "Now I'm really confused!" Instead of feeling smart and satisfied, some of us felt dumb and frustrated.

A similar potential twist occurred at the end of *Memento*. At its beginning, we're presented with a mystery: "Why is he killing this man?" "What's the truth behind this story?" Throughout the film, we wait for the truth. At the end, we almost learn it. Teddy explains some facts: Leonard killed his wife. Leonard also killed the guy who was responsible for the rape of his wife. In fact, Teddy took a photo of Leonard when he killed the rapist. But, along with this information that initially seems to clarify the story, Teddy also gives us confusing and contradictory information: Teddy tells Leonard that it doesn't matter whether the man Leonard killed was the right guy or not. Then, Teddy tells him that Sammy Jenkins didn't have a wife and that Leonard killed his own wife, who had diabetes. We see a flashback that shows Leonard with a syringe in his hand. In the next shot, we see him pinching her thigh. It looks as if Leonard is murdering his wife in the same way that Sammy Jenkins murded his wife. But the scene then looks as if he's just pinching her, not giving her insulin.

Teddy goes on to tell Leonard, "You're not a killer, Lenny. That's why you're so good at it," implying that Teddy has been using Leonard to kill various drug dealers that he wanted to get rid of by making Leonard think that each dealer was the one who raped his wife. Taken in the midst of so much conflicting third-act exposition, the truth of Teddy's assertions are unclear.

Since Teddy was deliberately obtuse, we don't know who to trust at the end. As a result, audience reaction was more intellectual than visceral. By the time we figure out one part of the twist, we've missed other important information.

Memento had opportunities for several well-defined twists—one right after the other: Sammy Jenkins didn't have a wife. Leonard killed his wife. Leonard already killed the murderer a year ago. Teddy has been using Leonard to get rid of drug dealers. But the film didn't play the movie's end as a twist—it simply piled up information. So many of us were left confused at the end.

Its unusual structure forced *Memento* to play out exposition in Act Three. All this information, which was given to us in a matter of minutes, was more than most of us could absorb all at once.

EXPOSING SECRETS & LIES

Not all secrets involve the twist. The film *Secrets & Lies* is about secrets and lies, but it's not a film based on twists. As it unfolds, it continually reveals new truths. It emphasizes the emotional tension caused by people carrying secrets and the uproar and upset that occur when secrets held for many years are finally revealed.

In the film, Cynthia has a secret. When she was sixteen, she had a baby out of wedlock who was given up for adoption. Her brother and sister-in-law know about the child, but her daughter, Roxanne, doesn't. Nor has Cynthia told anyone else.

This child is Hortense. When Hortense's adopted mother dies, she decides to find her birth mother. At the first turning point, Hortense talks to a social worker and begins her search during the first half of Act Two. Implicit in her search is a twist—Hortense is black, but she has a white mother. This could have been a very powerful twist, but it was not played as a twist. Instead, it was simply played as information. Hortense reads that her mother is white and asks the social worker if that could be a mistake. The social worker says, "Probably not."

A twist could have been created by not giving Hortense the information that her mother is white. Then, when Cynthia and Hortense meet, both of them—and the audience, too—would have a visceral reaction. Since Hortense already knew that her mother was white, this information destroyed a potentially dramatic emotional response from Hortense and the audience.

At the midpoint, Hortense and Cynthia meet, and Cynthia feels sympathetic to Hortense's search, but is quite sure that she couldn't possibly be her daughter. Then, we see Cynthia's reaction as it dawns on her that there had been a black man in her life. This moment also lets us know that Cynthia was a promiscuous fifteen-year-old who slept with several men during that period of time.

In the third act, the revelation of Cythia's secret brings out everyone else's secrets. Cynthia has harshly judged Monica, her sister-in-law, for years because Monica has no children and spends money to make up for that lack. It comes out that Monica can't have children, and that although her husband, Maurice, "loves her to bits," he admits that this secret has almost destroyed their relationship. Roxanne had no idea that her mother had another child, and that she has a half-sister. This secret has destroyed the relationship between Roxanne and Cynthia until it comes out, and this knowledge reconciles them. At the end, Hortense and Roxanne decide that it's "best to tell the truth—that way nobody gets hurt."

Re-watch *Secrets & Lies* and see whether you think the meeting between Cynthia and Hortense would have worked better at the first turning point rather than the midpoint. Until Cynthia and Hortense meet, the film presents parallel journeys, with parallel setups. Would you have preferred a faster setup, so the emotional journey could have had more time to be played out throughout Act Two? Or did you feel that the writer needed half the script to clearly establish these two worlds? Then, imagine the film with a twist at their meeting when Hortense and Cynthia and the audience all experience the twist at the same time.

Secrets and lies, like twist and turns, are created by the will of a character whose secret choices propel a story forward, create drama, provide an undercurrent of conflict, and move a story to a resolution that will reveal the secret. The truth is told, the characters find some sort of reconciliation, and the audience gets it and is satisfied.

6

What's It Really About?

A film is a journey, not only into the world of the story, but into the world of ideas. Great films contain great themes. We feel that a great film, in some way, is talking about our lives, our themes, our issues. Through it, we gain insight into how our world works and how our lives work. Sometimes we experience deeper emotions than we feel in our everyday lives. It's as if a film's ideas, expressed through character and conflict, create a deeper connection with our own lives. Sometimes we make new life decisions as a result of seeing a film, or affirm decisions that we already made.

Most films carry fairly simple ideas: finding integrity, establishing justice, overcoming evil, finding love. Some films grapple with more complex ideas—such as the ambiguity of good found in *Schindler's List* and the search for authenticity found in *American Beauty*.

How does a writer choose themes to explore in a script? From life—the source of drama. The more we understand the patterns and processes of our own lives, the more we can create deep and insightful films.

WHAT IS A GREAT WRITER?

The great writer is part philosopher, part psychologist, part theologian. As a philosopher, the writer poses the questions: What's the meaning of these events? What's my interpretation of the lives of these characters? What's the purpose of this story? Does it matter? Do I see the world through the eyes of a realist? An idealist? An optimist? A pessimist? A humanist? Is my view of life dark? Light? Comedic? Casual? Serious? Is human nature inherently good? Inherently bad? Both? Can good triumph over evil? How much free will do we have? Are we doomed to repeat history or do we have a choice? How do I express my philosophy of life so that my work has its own artistic voice?

As a psychologist, a writer asks, "What motivates my characters? Why do they do what they do? What moves them? What do they fear? What do they seek in life? What do they need? What do they want with all their heart? How far will they go to get what they want? How functional or dysfunctional are they? What are the dynamics of their relationships with others?"

As a theologian, a writer asks, "Where is the good and where is the evil in my story? Do my characters get transformed or redeemed? If so, how? Must we always suffer the consequences of our actions? Can we find redemption, forgiveness, and transformation? What values are expressed through my story and characters and images? Is there a spiritual layer to my characters' lives? How can it be conveyed?"

All of these elements—the philosophical, the psychological, and the theological—can carry a story's theme. Although most writers will emphasize one above the other, great films contain some aspects of all three disciplines.

For instance, *Places in the Heart* offers a theological theme with a value system that emphasizes community, sharing, and helping each other during the Great Depression. Its psychological theme shows a clear, realistic portrait of a woman overcoming her racism and her limits, because her determination and love of her children moves her to do almost anything to save her family. It shows an optimistic view of life: Goodness prevails in spite of difficult circumstances.

Amadeus shows the psychology of a man, Salieri, consumed by envy, obsessed with his own mediocrity, and confused by the greatness of Mozart. In his theology, he sees God as the enemy. The film emphasizes Salieri's warped theology—in particular, his belief in an unfair God, which led to his attempted suicide. Salieri blames God for his mediocrity and recognizes God's gift to Mozart, whose compositions seem to him like dictation from God. The film's theological aspect is reinforced by showing Salieri confessing to a priest and burning a crucifix to show his rejection of God. Philosophically, this period of history was a time when some began to move from a theological view of life to a more philosophical and rational-scientific view. The characters in *Amadeus* show three different aspects of a response to God. Salieri is the person who turns his back on God, Mozart shows a more humanist, individualistic philsophy, and Franz Joseph shows the more practical philosophical approach to life.

A Beautiful Mind is a psychological portrait of a man with a mental illness. The film's philosophical/theological layer shows the beautiful mind surrounded by demons.

The theology found in such films as *The Thin Red Line* and *Ghost* and the *Star Wars* films follows the soul or "the force" that many consider an intrinsic part of our lives. *Ghost* affirms this force as part of the afterlife. *The Thin Red Line* talks about us as being "one big soul." *Apocalypse Now* recognizes the pervasive presence of evil:

CHEF

This is evil — evil, Captain. We're all gonna die here.

WILLARD

I know.

Other films look at such theological themes as temptation, the striving for power, the search for God. Some films ask, "Under what circumstances are we willing to sell our souls?" We can find theological themes in *Bugsy, Nixon, Magnolia, Quiz Show,* and *L.A. Confidential.*

Many films are driven by a particular philosophical system. Mythologist Pamela Jaye Smith discusses some of these philosophical systems in her mythology classes and has shared the following ideas with me for this book:

> Films such as *Driving Miss Daisy, Erin Brockovich, Mississippi Burning,* and *Titanic* show a philosophy that is almost Marxist in the way it looks at the perpetual class struggle of the haves versus the have-nots.

> Films such as *Unforgiven, The English Patient, The Usual Suspects,* and *The Silence of the Lambs* have echoes of existential philosophy with its emphasis on despair and hopelessness over our human condition.

> Some films express the philosophy of the individual acting under the motive of the greatest good for the greatest number. In films such as *Braveheart, The Mission, The Insider, Schindler's List,* and *Elizabeth,* we see the hero sacrificing himself or herself for something bigger, for a greater good.

> There are stories that show that the ends are more important than the means. In films such as *Pride and Prejudice, The End of the Affair, Traffic, Goodfellas, The Crying Game,* and *The Godfather* movies, we see that the practical outcome is more important than high ideals.

> Some films draw upon Eastern philosophy, with its fluid time and flexible reality. We can see the influence of Buddhism and Taoism in such films as *The Matrix, Run Lola Run, The Sixth Sense, Crouching Tiger, Hidden Dragon,* and *Sliding Doors.*

> And many successful films have followed, perhaps unwittingly, the quote of the German philosopher Nietzsche, who observed, "That which does not kill us makes us stronger." We see this individualism and a life-affirming heroic stance in such films as *The Lord*

*of the Rings: Fellowship of the Ring, Saving Private
Ryan, Pulp Fiction,* and *Gladiator.*

THE EVER-PRESENT IDENTITY THEME

Some years ago, producer-director Sydney Pollack told me
that every film that he makes is a love story. In *Tootsie,* he
explored love and friendship. In *They Shoot Horses, Don't They?*
he explored the burdens and crises of love. In *Out of Africa,*
he explored love and possession.

I was intrigued by how Pollack used an overriding theme
for all of his films. As a result, I began to look for themes that
seem to appear in most films, and then to look for different
expressions of these themes. As I thought about how to discuss the concept of theme for this book, I realized that most
themes are, in some way, about identity. Some themes are
about finding or realizing one's identity. This idea is found in
many coming-of-age stories, from *Dirty Dancing* to *Porky's*
to *My Brilliant Career* to *Risky Business* to *Dead Poets Society.* Some themes are about holding on to one's identity despite oppression. This idea is found in *One Flew Over the
Cuckoo's Nest, The Cider House Rules, Erin Brockovich, Forrest
Gump, Braveheart,* and *Do the Right Thing.* Some themes are
about finding one's identity within a certain career, sport, or
art form. We find this in *Pollock, Shine,* and *Rocky.* Some
themes are about claiming one's identity in spite of forces
that threaten it, such as illness (*Magnolia, One True Thing, A
Beautiful Mind*) or prison (*The Green Mile, Shawshank Redemption*) or being adopted by a dog instead of a pig (*Babe*).

If we look at some of the Academy Award winners of the
1980s and 1990s, we can see an identity theme shimmering
through the many philosophical, theological, and/or psychological ideas.

A Beautiful Mind: A man maintains his identity despite his
mental illness and manages to contribute brilliant ideas in
spite of his limitations.

American Beauty: A man goes through a mid-life identity crisis, trying to find authenticity in an inauthentic world.

Shakespeare in Love: Shakespeare needs his muse to write—an ability that defines his identity. He almost loses this ability because of writer's block, but he regains it through love. This film also explores the identity crisis of Viola, who wants to avoid the identity her family and society imposes on her as a bartered bride. She alters her identity by posing as a boy actor, but is found out, so she eventually takes on the identity assigned to her by her social status.

Titanic: This is a coming-of-age story about a woman who discovers who she really is and what she really wants in life through her relationship with a young man who already knows his own identity, but her family and social peers object to their relationship.

Braveheart: William Wallace never doubts his own identity. His strong confidence in his own identity and his patriotism brings about changes in others, such as Robert the Bruce and the Scottish soldiers who join him in battle. Over the course of the film, he strengthens his identity as a Scot. This, in turn, affects the national identity of Scotland.

Forrest Gump: Forrest maintains his integrity and identity despite his mental limits.

Schindler's List: Ambivalent about his own goodness, Schindler becomes a good man in spite of himself.

Unforgiven: A gunslinger and killer who has found a new identity temporarily goes back to his old life, but finds his old life no longer fits him.

THEME AS MOVEMENT

Notice that in all the films just cited above, identity is defined by movement toward a truer identity. They're about the seeking, discovering, maintaining, or realizing one's identity. These are verbs, action words.

You've undoubtedly heard the saying "A rolling stone gathers no moss." I say, "A rolling theme gathers ideas, associations, character, and story." A theme develops and builds. It *moves* throughout an entire film.

American Beauty is a good example of a film with a theme that moves throughout its story, clearly articulating psychological and theological issues. We might define its theme as: A man confronts his mid-life crisis, in a desire to live an authentic life. Notice the action word "confronts," which also implies a context—a mid-life crisis—and a goal, the authentic life.

In his book *The Art of Dramatic Writing*, Lajos Egri defines theme as a premise that is proven by the story. He says that a premise is not a static statement, but a phrase that expresses the movement of a theme from the beginning of a drama to its end.

He defines *Macbeth*'s premise as "ruthless ambition leads to destruction." I like how Egri defines this premise since the phrase implies three acts. The first act introduces a man with ruthless ambition. The third act shows his destruction. And the second act shows the process by which ruthless ambition leads to destruction.

If we apply Egri's concept to *American Beauty*, the premise might be: Confronting the inauthentic life leads to struggle and redemption.

A writer who chose this theme would have to prove it by first showing an inauthentic life (Act One), then showing the protagonist struggling and confronting his life (Act Two), and then showing the protagonist's redemption at the end (Act Three).

I have difficulty applying Egri's concept of theme to every film. When I consult on a script, I occasionally work with his idea of premise, which I sometimes find to be the best way to get a handle on a writer's theme. More often, however, I work with the idea of theme as a movement to a *more desired state*. Considering *American Beauty*, I might say it's a story about seeking and expressing one's integrity or finding authenticity or finding the meaning in life. Often, I try to express a theme in a variety of ways, so a writer can decide which articulation of a theme best resonates with what s/he wants to say in the story.

In the early stages of writing, it's not unusual for a script's theme to be unclear, vague, or abstract. When a theme is clear, it guides a writer, who can then make sure that every scene and the story's overall movement expresses the idea.

HOW IS A THEME EXPRESSED?

A theme is expressed through dialogue, story, character choices, and images.

Most good films will tell the audience its theme in a very concise and memorable sentence. In *Ghost*, Sam states the theme at the end of a film, as he faces the light: "It's so amazing, Moll ... the love inside ... You take it with you."

The theme need not be expressed by the main character. In *Ghost*, the villain, Carl, expresses part of the theme when he tells Molly, "You have to remember the love you felt. That's what's real. You have to remember how good Sam was. How much he loved you. You were everything to him, Molly, you were his life ..."

<pre>
                    MOLLY
        I feel so alone.

                    CARL
        You're not alone.
</pre>

In *Dead Poets Society*, the theme about finding the balance between creativity and conformity is revealed when Keating tells Charlie, "That was a pretty lame stunt you pulled."

<pre>
                  CHARLIE
        I thought you'd like it ... sucking
        the marrow out of life.

                  KEATING
        Sucking the marrow out of life does
        not mean choking on the bone. There
</pre>

> is a time for daring and a time for
> caution. The wise man understands
> which is called for.

Expressions of theme through dialogue can occur anywhere in the script, although they are most apt to occur toward the middle or end of Act Two, as a reinforcement to the meaning of the unfolding story. Keating's statement of theme comes near the second turning point. The theme in *Ghost* is expressed in the climactic scene.

In *American Beauty*, thematic dialogue weaves its way throughout the entire film. Since the film is played as a flashback, the expression of the theme begins and ends the film. At the opening:

> LESTER (V.O.)
> I feel like I've been in a coma for
> about 20 years and I'm just now
> waking up.

The story then communicates the theme of his crisis of meaning as he takes action to try to find a more authentic life.

> LESTER
> Janie, today I quit my job. I also
> told my boss to fuck himself and
> then blackmailed him for almost
> $60,000. Pass the asparagus.

And, at the film's end, after he's been killed, he expresses the theme again.

> LESTER (V.O.)
> I guess I could be pretty pissed
> off about what happened to me ...
> but it's hard to stay mad when
> there's so much beauty in the world
> ... it flows through me like rain
> and I can't feel anything but
> gratitude for every single moment
> of my stupid little life ... You

> have no idea what I'm talking
> about, I'm sure ... but don't worry
> ... you will someday.

Spiderman states its theme at both the first turning point and the climax: "With great power comes great responsibility." Although this might seem like a static statement rather than a moving theme, the story actually shows a boy *understanding* his great power, *learning* to be responsible. At the end, he chooses not to put the girl above his responsibility and walks off, preparing us for the sequel.

Tootsie plays with the theme of male versus female. Les, who has become very interested in Dorothy, talks about his views of men and women toward the end of Act Two.

> LES
>
> I can remember years ago there was
> none of this talk about what a
> woman was, what a man was ... Now
> there's all these experiments to
> find out how much you should be
> like the sex you're not so we can
> be all the same, but we're just
> not, you know? Not on a farm,
> that's for sure. Bulls are bulls,
> and roosters don't try to lay eggs.

And at the end of a film, Michael explains clearly to Julie what he's learned about men and women, and about love and friendship.

> MICHAEL
>
> You know — I was a better man with
> you as a woman with you than I ever
> was as a man with a woman. You know
> what I mean? I learned a few things
> about myself being Dorothy. I just
> have to learn to do it without the
> dress. Look, the really hard part's
> over — we're already best friends.

At the end of *Memento*, Teddy tells Leonard about the meaning of the events in his life: "You're living a dream, kid. A dead wife to pine for and a sense of purpose to your life. A romantic quest which you wouldn't end even if I wasn't in the picture."

And Leonard responds, recognizing that this is where he finds meaning: "I have to believe in the world outside my own mind. I have to believe that my actions still have meaning, even though I can't remember them. I have to believe that when my eyes are closed, the world's still there."

In *The People vs. Larry Flynt*, Larry expresses the theme at the end: "If the First Amendment will protect a scumbag like me, then it can protect all of you." And the film proves that the First Amendment protected him.

In Act Three of *Secrets & Lies*, Maurice gives a speech that reveals the theme:

```
                MAURICE
    Secrets and lies — we're all in
    pain. Why can't we share our pain?
    I've spent my entire life trying to
    make people happy and the three
    people I love the most in the world
    hate each other's guts. I'm in the
    middle and I can't take it anymore.
    You want to find the truth, you
    have to be prepared to suffer the
    consequences.
```

In *The Usual Suspects*, Verbal states the theme at the film's end: "The greatest trick the devil ever pulled was convincing the world he didn't exist." The film shows that Keyser Soze has pulled it off.

Reversing the theme

Sometimes a writer plays with a theme by having a character express an opposing idea. We learn the theme through its negation rather than through its positive expression.

In *Schindler's List*, Goeth says about his maid, "The most merciful thing I could do would be to take her out in the woods and shoot her painlessly in the head." Obviously, a writer doesn't believe this is merciful. But since the theme explores the ambivalence of Good, Goeth's words about an evil act highlights the overall idea of good versus evil.

Memento's theme concerns the importance of memory, the quest for life's meaning in spite of tragedy, and specifically Leonard's inability to create a new life and a new identity. Leonard tells Teddy that facts are more important than memory. "Memory's not perfect. It's not even that good. Ask the police; eyewitness testimony is unreliable. The cops ... collects facts, make notes, draw conclusions. Facts, not memories; that's how they investigate ... Memories can be changed or distorted and they're irrelevant if you have the facts." But at the end, Leonard clings to memories, not facts. And, by the end, we've seen how important memory is as he tries to rebuild his life without it.

Toxic themes and transforming themes

We often assume that all film themes will be about positive aspects of the human condition. We assume that, somehow, as the protagonist goes through the story, the actions and changes and ideas implicit in the storyline will eventually show the best of humanity. Yet, it's not unusual for a writer to unconsciously project a theme that may be morally toxic, destructive, and sometimes even contrary to what the writer thinks is being said.

Morally toxic themes might include: "Might makes right." "The female is an object, without the same abilities, skills, or value as the man." "Non-whites are expendable." "Anyone over age fifty is useless and not necessary to our civilization." "Violence will win out in the end."

Themes change as culture changes. An old theme that is morally toxic in today's world may, however, find itself embedded in a writer's stories. Folklorist Karen Dietz notes some toxic story themes versus less-toxic alternatives:

- Sex is an itch to scratch versus sex is sacred.
- Redemption through violence versus redemption through peace.
- The rights of the individual versus stories of community.
- Reverence for the personality versus reverence for character and integrity.
- Consumerism versus simplicity.
- Dominance versus diversity.

Many Academy Award-nominated films contain underlying themes that may have not been what the writer intended. Although I suspect that the writer and director of *Braveheart* thought that they were creating a theme of justice, I found themes of revenge that seem to say that killing is justified when the other person makes the first strike and a theme that says a good defense is a strong offense.

In *The Usual Suspects,* the theme seems to say that lying is all right if you can get away with it.

A case might be made that films like *Natural Born Killers* and *Bonnie and Clyde* glamorize the criminal lifestyle and tell us, "It was fun while it lasted."

A writer needs to be careful to make sure that a theme is truly communicating what s/he hopes is being commuicated. "I think the positive stories are richer than their alternatives," says Karen Dietz. "There's more that we can learn from them. They're more dimensional, and they create more positive effects in the audience."

Theme expressed through the story

Scripts express their themes through their writers' story choices. If story choices are arbitrary, the theme will be vague and muddled. If the story choices are clear and well worked-out, the theme becomes clear.

In *American Beauty*, each story beat tells us something more about Lester's desire to change his meaningless life. He tells off his boss, quits his job, takes a non-thinking job, re-awakens his erotic self through his infatuation with a cheer-leader, builds up his physical body to find his sexually attrac-tive self, tries to awaken his love with his wife, tries new behaviors (such as drugs with the next-door neighbor), finds and affirms his moral self by choosing not to sleep with the cheerleader, and, at the end, sees life as beautiful.

L.A. Confidential has a storyline that conveys the theme of corruption battling against integrity. We see Dudley mak-ing speeches about cleaning up the town while beating up the guys who are making his town dirty. We see him seem-ingly investigating a murder, only to shoot Jack when Jack begins to delve too deeply into the case. The world that's created is one of betrayals and secrets. The film has specific story beats about that which is hidden, that which is compro-mised, and that which is finally revealed.

Theme expressed through character

Sometimes a theme is expressed by creating an either/or state-ment—exploring a theme by creating characters to represent different aspects of its theme. Although this technique is rare, it worked well in *One Flew Over the Cuckoo's Nest*, which is about liberation versus tyranny. It also worked well in *Dead Poets Society*, which is about creativity versus conformity, and in *Sense and Sensibility*, which is about inappropriate/impetu-ous love versus sensible and "sense-able" love.

In *Dead Poets Society*, each character represents either the push of conformity or the pull of creativity. The school's prin-cipal represents unchanging tradition, which isn't bad until it impedes creativity. Todd represents the person transformed by creativity, and by the film's end, he's learned to stand up for what he believes. Charlie represents the person who be-lieves that creativity encourages chaos. Neil represents the boy who can't hold on to his creativity against the force of his father's dreams for him. Neil feels there's only one way to respond to the squelching of his creativity—suicide. The par-ents, as a group, represent the conformist culture that wants their sons to be doctors and lawyers. However, each parent is shaded differently. Neil's father wants him to be a doctor, and to take the opportunities he never had. Neil's mother is sympathetic to her son's desires, but conforms to her husband's decisions. Todd's parents want him to follow the rules. Other parents just want their children to do well and not jeopardize the prestige of the school. Keating represents stability and wisdom. He understands both the pitfalls and the possibilities of creativity.

In *Sense and Sensibility*, several characters represent inappropriate love—the love that Marianne has for the dashing Mr. Willoughby and the love Lucy has for Edward's supposed position and money. We see the appropriate and sensible and true love through the characters of Edward and Elinor and Brandon's love for Marianne.

Similar contrasts are found in *American Beauty*'s theme of authenticity versus inauthenticity. Lester searches for the authentic life. His inauthentic wife is driven by the culture-bound desire for perfection and prestige. The cheerleader pretends she's someone other than who she is. The father next door denies his homosexuality. The oppressed wife next door is defined solely by her husband and has no identity of her own. The daughter and next-door neighbor boy band together to try to figure out their identities in the midst of these dysfunctional characters.

In these films mentioned above, it seems that the writer is expressing his viewpoint through the voice of the main character. If you want to know what writer Tom Schulman thinks about creativity versus conformity, listen to what Keating says about it. If you want to know what writer Emma Thompson thinks about true love, look at how everything works itself out in *Sense and Sensibility* and you'll know where she stands.

Theme expressed through image

A theme can be be carried by a film's visuals. In a film about oppression, we might see images of darkness, of constrained spaces, of dead-ends, and of captivity. In a film about freedom, we might see open spaces, roads moving to a mysterious far-off place, contrasting light and dark images to show the darkness that the character wishes to escape and the light that pulls the character toward another life. In a film about inauthenticity, we might see mirrors that show distorted reality or translucent windows that don't clearly show us the real world.

American Beauty uses a variety of images to convey its theme about the search for the authentic life. We see the perfect red American Beauty roses picked by Lester's wife, who wears gardening clogs that match her gardening sheers (Lester tells us this is no accident), attesting to her uptight life of proper appearances. The dewy rose petals that cover the naked body of the cheerleader represent Lester's desire to start again, to be spontaneous, to express himself freely.

Various images of voyeurism express the film's theme: showing lives through filters, seen through the camera lens, through curtains, through windows.

Together, these elements not only make statements about the mid-life crisis, but show Lester's movement from the inauthentic life to the authentic life.

When working with theme as image, ask yourself, "What does this theme look like? How can I show an abstraction through a visual? Do I want to work with big spaces to show the desire for a larger world, such as in *Dances with Wolves, Out of Africa,* or *The Mission*? Do I want to work with small spaces to show a constricted world, such as in *The Green Mile, A Soldier's Story, Remains of the Day,* or *The Full Monty*? Do I want to work with the contrasts of constricted spaces and open spaces to show a character's longing to have a room with a view and the desire to be king of the world, as in *Titanic*?"

Since film is a visual medium, images are the most powerful way to convey a theme. Although some images will be created by the director, most need to be in the script so that the director has a clear guide to help strategize the execution of the story.

Theme expressed through metaphor

Sometimes a theme is presented as a metaphor. In *Silence of the Lambs*, there isn't any place where a writer directly tells us that facing evil leads to conquering evil (which might be one expression of a film's premise) or that intuition leads to answers. However, around the film's midpoint, Clarice talks about trying to save the lambs from being slaughtered.

>   DR. LECTER
> What's your worst memory of child-
> hood?
>   (she hesitates)
>
> Quicker than that. I'm not inter-
> ested in your worst <u>invention</u>.
>
>
>   CLARICE
> The death of my father.
>
>
>   DR. LECTER
> Tell me. Don't lie, or I'll know.

She then tells Hannibal that after the death of her father she went to live with her mother's cousin and her husband on a ranch in Montana. They had horses and sheep.

>   CLARICE
> One morning, I just - ran away...
>
>
>   DR. LECTER
> Not "Just," Clarice. What set you
> off?
>
>
>   CLARICE
> I heard a strange sound...
>
>
>   DR. LECTER
> What was it?
>
>
>   CLARICE
> I don't know. I went to look...

                    CLARICE
Screaming: Some kind of - screaming. Like a child's voice ... I
crept up to the barn ... I was so
scared to look inside, but I had to
...

                    DR. LECTER
And what did you see, Clarice?

                    CLARICE
The lambs were screaming ...

                    DR. LECTER
They were slaughtering the spring
lambs?

                    CLARICE
Yes ... they were screaming.

                    DR. LECTER
So you ran away….

                    CLARICE
No. First I tried to free them ... I
opened the gate of their pen — but
they wouldn't run. They just stood
there, confused. They wouldn't run.

                    DR. LECTER
But you could. You did.

                    CLARICE
I took one lamb. And I ran away, as
fast as I could ... I had no food
or water. It was very cold. I
thought — if I can even save just
one ... but he got so heavy. So
heavy ... I didn't get more than a
few miles before the sheriff's car

    found me. The rancher was so angry
    he sent me to live at the Lutheran
    orphange in Bozeman. I never saw
    the ranch again ...

               DR. LECTER
    But what became of your lamb?

            (no response)

    Clarice...? You still wake up some-
    times, don't you? Wake up in the
    dark, with the lambs screaming?

               CLARICE
    Yes ...

               DR. LECTER
    Do you think if you saved
    Catherine, you could make them
    stop...? Do you think if Catherine
    lives you won't wake up in the dark
    ever again? To the screaming of the
    lambs? <u>Do</u> you?

And at the end of a film, after Hannibal has escaped, he tele-
phones Clarice and says: "Your flock is still for now, Clarice,
but not forever. You'll have to earn it again and again. You
know, this blessed silence. For you, there will always be other
lambs, on other nights ..."

    Through this dialogue, we understand why Clarice became
an FBI agent, what motivates her, what she desires, and why
she's willing to put herself in such danger to continue to save
the innocents.

Character as metaphor

Sometimes a film's major character is a metaphor. In *One Flew
Over the Cuckoo's Nest*, McMurphy has been compared to a
Christ figure, representing Christ the Liberator, who comes
into an alienated world, empowers those without power, is

killed for his deeds, and is resurrected in the lives of others who find freedom.

Just as one can create a metaphoric Christ figure who isn't meant to be the actual character of Jesus Christ, one can create a Moses figure who represents freedom and liberation from oppression and takes others to a "promised land." Similarly, one could create a character who carries the symbols and resonances of the compassionate and enlightened Buddha. Some writers might find their metaphorical characters in mythology, recreating such tales as the hero's journey or the Brunhilda myth or Krishna's journey. As writers delve deeply into the inner worlds of their characters, they can find many ways of creating characters who resonate with some of the deep universal themes of the world's religion and mythology.

THE THEME HAS TO FIT THE AUDIENCE

Themes tend to be age-specific. The problems that we encounter at one stage of our lives are different than what we encounter at another age. A critically and commercially successful film explores the issues that are relevant to the age of its main character and issues that are relevant to the age of its intended core audience. There's a reason why the coming-of-age stories often do well—we've all come of age and, therefore, on some level, we know the film is really about us.

In the 1950s, Erik Erikson wrote a seminal work, *Childhood and Society*. It's about the stages that we go through in our lives as we mature. Other books have also investigated the life stages of adults, such as Gail Sheehey's *Passages,* Daniel Levinson's work on the male mid-life crisis in *Seasons of a Man's Life,* and Maggie Scarf's exploration of women's development in *Pressure Points in the Lives of Women.* I have found these books helpful in understanding the themes that people encounter at specific stages in their lives. When consulting, I often refer back to these ideas to help writers strengthen these themes in their stories.

Childhood

Allmost every film about children deals with issues of trust, self-esteem, and a sense of belonging. In most films about children, the film's journey builds the child's confidence and, at the end, the child has gained a greater sense of self-esteem and belonging (e.g., *Home Alone, War Games, The Last Starfighter, Spy Kids, E.T.*).

They achieve this growth by overcoming the resistances that can come from parents, teachers, neighbors, relatives, the bad guys out there, and culture. The inherent drama of childhood comes from exploring the adult world's resistance to the child's maturing self and the action the child takes to overcome that resistance.

The child deals with these resistances in two ways. The child may turn inward when faced with a problem and blame him or herself, deciding that s/he's no good. This can lead to depression and low self-confidence. Or the child can project the problem outward onto others, deciding that they're no good. As a result, the child can become rebellious or delinquent, often living outside the law (e.g., *Natural Born Killers*).

The problems children confront not only affect them, but also other members of their families. A story about a child's lack of confidence can also be a story about an overburdened mother who is battered or neglected. Her lack of confidence may be transferred to the child. The story might be about a father who neglects his children or abuses his children, leading to a child's low self-esteem. Such a father might serve to express the theme about a man who escapes his own problems by controlling others, or through work or womanizing.

The teen years

Almost every teenage film will, in one way or another, deal with the idea of identity, since the teen years and early twenties are about finding ourselves. Who are we? What do we want to *do* when we grow up? Who do we want to *be* when we grow up?

A teen-oriented film might be about the coming of age of sexual identity (*Risky Business,* the teenagers in *American Beauty, Boys Don't Cry, Dangerous Beauty, Fast Times at Ridgemont High*), about finding love (*Titanic, Clueless*), about finding one's creative self in the midst of a conformist culture (*Dead Poets Society*), or about finding one's individuality in a culture that has already defined who you are, including who you're supposed to marry and what you're supposed to be (*A Room with a View, Titanic, The Cider House Rules*).

Young adulthood

If young people don't find their identities, they may find themselves drifting, in spite of their considerable talents (*Good Will Hunting*) or in bad or mediocre marriages (*The Bridges of Madison County*) or getting addicted to drugs or alcohol (*Leaving Las Vegas*) or committing a crime (*The Talented Mister Ripley*) or committing suicide (*Dead Poets Society*).

Films depicitng characters in their late teens through thirties will usually deal with issues of love and intimacy. Intimacy might be defined as love, sexuality, friendship, or community. Both *When Harry Met Sally* and *Tootsie* explore love that begins as friendship. Some films deal with the choices that love demands of us, such as choosing someone who our parents wouldn't want us to choose (*Titanic*) or choosing duty above love (*Elizabeth*) or having to leave a loved one (*Shakespeare in Love*).

Many films that cater to audiences in their twenties and thirties are about success and achievement. *The Cider House Rules* is about a young man's desire to be a doctor, *Rocky* is about finding one's talents, *Wall Street* is about realizing that success does not preclude integrity, and *The Full Monty* is about finding success in whatever way one can.

Success themes often are about finding success in the world's eyes. The major character might be fulfilling his/her own dream, but if the world doesn't affirm the dream, that dream may seem unimportant. In most of these films, we expect some public acknowledgement of a character's achievements. Clarice receives an award at the end of *The Silence of the Lambs*. John Nash wins the Nobel Prize in *A Beautiful Mind*. The first *Star Wars* film ends with an award ceremony.

Some films deal with the conflict between family and career (*One True Thing, Melvin's Room*) or between the pull of materialism and fame versus the desire for integrity (*Jerry Maguire, Magnolia, Quiz Show*).

Most of the films mentioned above use their main storylines to define a goal and their subplots to explore intimacy and relationships.

Twenties through forties

During their twenties, thirties, and forties, individuals often must deal with the theme of spirituality versus materialism. Films based on such a theme take a stand for what their characters consider important in life, and the characters usually choose to negate life's material comforts in favor of affirming such spiritual values as integrity, social conscienceness, good relationships, and self-sacrifice. We can see these themes in such films as *Seven Years in Tibet, Gandhi, Norma Rae,* and *Erin Brockovich*.

Fifties through eighties

Erik Erikson ended *Childhood and Society* with a discussion of integrity versus despair. We might define integrity as holding to one's ethical or moral identity, even though strong forces threaten to knock one off his or her authentic self. Erikson believed that the issue of integrity is something that everyone has to confront as they get older: What has one made of one's life? What has one contributed? Have one's talents been actualized?

Whereas success in the middle years focuses on whether the world recognizes one's success, integrity relates more to how an individiual affirms their life, whether or not they've lived by the world's definition of success. Stories abound about people who seem to have it all according to a materialistic definition of success, but have compromised their integrity to reach a materialistic goal. In some cases, they may lose their fame, respect, money, and power when they're found out.

Erikson sees the issue of integrity versus despair as a particularly strong concern of those in their sixties; however, integrity themes can fit characters of almost any age.

Film history is filled with integrity-themed movies. They can speak to us at almost any age. From the time that we're in grade school we're taught not to cheat, not to tattle, not to steal. We're taught to choose honesty above dishonesty and not to give in to temptation and to stand up for the underdog. Throughout our lives, our integrity is tested. It's a major character issue. In fact, looking over Academy Award-nominated films, it's not unusual to see one or more integrity themes every year. Recent years have brought us: *A Beautiful Mind, The Lord of the Rings, Erin Brockovich, Gladiator, Traffic, The Insider, The Green Mile, American Beauty, The Cider House Rules, Elizabeth, Saving Private Ryan, L.A. Confidential.*

Old age

As we age and approach death, another issue grows in importance. I call it reconciliation versus regret. We want to resolve past hurts, heal relationships, and overcome alienation with connection.

In *Magnolia*, the dying father recognizes that he has to reconcile with his son, in order to affirm his own integrity. In *Marvin's Room*, the family needs reconciliation. In *On Golden Pond*, three generations of characters reach reconciliation with one another.

Toward the end of life

Although the reconciliation theme might be found as one nears death, there is also another theme that is apparent as death creeps ever nearer. I call this theme "rage versus mellow acceptance." When my mother was declining, I spent time at her nursing home, where I noticed how many people were enraged at their situation and took out that rage on their children, the nurses, and the staff. I sensed that the enraged patients had not handled their basic life issues when they faced them at earlier stages in their lives. As a result, they were furious, because they believed life had cheated them or passed them by or that somehow they had blown it. On the other hand, I also met people in their declining years who seemed to face the end of their lives with mellow acceptance. Both of my parents became mellow, grateful, and in a gentle state of surrender toward the end of their lives.

I have not seen any films that deal with this final aspect of life, but I hope to in the future. This might change as more successful writers reach the stage of their lives when they observe how their parents respond to the end of their lives and decide to explore this in film.

Erikson says that if we don't handle our life themes when they naturally come up, they will continue to come up in our lives, demanding that we pay attention to them. It's not unusual to see a character in a film handling several themes at once. Todd, in *Dead Poets Society*, is forced to confront issues of self-esteem, belonging, identity, and integrity because he had never handled his self-esteem issues as a child, and had not yet handled his identity issues as a teenager. Charlie, in *Rain Man*, confronts his issues of belonging, success and achievement, intimacy, and integrity all in the same film, since he still carries with him the pain of a childhood in which he didn't belong. A character who's dying may be forced to deal with all of these issues at once.

FINDING THE ISSUE RELATED TO THE THEME

If a film has a well-worked-out theme, audiences discuss it. It raises psychological and social issues.

Since drama is about conflict, every theme contains a positive (what the theme looks like when it's been resolved) and a negative (the problem that comes up if it's not confronted and resolved).

Think of *Amadeus* and its exploration of mediocrity. How many of you have wondered if you were as creative as you would like to be? Have you ever felt competitive with those who received more awards, money, or recognition than you did? Have you ever wondered if some other writer was blessed or lucky and you weren't?

After watching *Dead Poets Society*, have you wondered if you've seized the day? Have you made any different decisions about your life because of the inspiration of Keating? Did a film make you think of teachers who had inspired you?

In the Bedroom presents an ethical dilemma. Was killing the perpetrator the only alternative? How do you handle your moral and psychological dilemmas?

Although many stories seem to be primarily about individual issues, they can also resonate with social issues, such as abuse, oppression, discrimination, sexism, racism, ageism, or pollution. Such films set up the relationship between the theme that's being explored and an individual or social issue that needs to be resolved.

Although *Thelma & Louise* seems to be about individual issues of freedom and oppression, a closer look at it reveals its concern with such social issues as feminism, justice, rape, and how individuals and social services and law enforcement handle violence and abuse. A film may lead us to ask, Should they have killed themselves? What choices did they have in a society that is sexist and had harmed Louise in the past?

Think of *Schindler's List*, set in the social context of Nazi Germany, with its themes about the ambivalence of Good and the impact one's life can have on others. Have you felt the pull of money and the easy life, issues that may conflict with your sense of compassion and selfless action?

Many films explore social issues: pollution in *Erin Brockovich;* corruption in *Wall Street, Jerry Maguire,* and *L.A. Confidential;* oppression in *Gladiator;* abortion in *The Cider House Rules;* politics in *In the Name of the Father.*

We might consider the relationship of theme and social and individual issues through the following chart:

THEME/IDEA	ISSUE	EXAMPLES
If a person doesn't find his/her identity and conforms or has low self-esteem, it can lead to . . .	withdrawal from others . . . or rebelliousness.	The child in *The Sixth Sense,* Will in *Good Will Hunting, Natural Born Killers*
If a person doesn't resolve intimacy issues, the result may be	alienation and/or depression, drugs and/or alcoholism, or crime	*As Good As It Gets, Once We Were Warriors, The Verdict, Who Framed Roger Rabbit?, Chicago*
If a person doesn't resolve integrity issues, s/he may someday face a moment when s/he must find a self-identity and stand up against corruption, or otherwise stoop to	cheating, corporate crime, or war profiteering	*Quiz Show, Wall Street, Schindler's List*

Think about some of your favorite films and see where they would fit within this chart.

THE THEME THAT SUMS UP THE POINT OF THE STORY

Sometimes, toward the end of a story, there is the final, summing-up statement.

The President in *Dave* sums up what he learned, affirming the values of self-sacrifice and responsibility:

> DAVE
>
> I forgot that I was hired to do a job for you and that it was just a temporary job at that ...I forgot that I had two hundred and fifty million people who were paying me to make their lives a little better and I didn't live up to my part of the bargain ...See, there are certain things you should expect from a President. I ought to care more about you than I do about me ...I ought to care more about what's right than I do about what's popular ...I ought to be willing to give this whole thing up for something I believe in, because if I'm not ...If I'm not ...then I don't belong here in the first place.

In *Moonstruck*, Ronny sums up the film by telling us all that we really need to know about love.

> RONNY
>
> Love don't make things nice. It ruins everything. It breaks your heart, it makes things a mess. We're not here to make things perfect. Snowflakes are perfect. The stars are perfect. Not us. Not us! We are here to ruin ourselves and break our hearts and love the wrong people and die! ...Come upstairs with me and get in my bed!

Ideas in films are not abstract. They're expressed through the story, through the characters, and through the images. Great drama begins with a writer who is clear about the themes being explored in his or her film. Then the writer looks for ways to express these ideas. In a film, one of those ways is through images.

7

Show, Don't Tell

A great screenwriter is a visual thinker who sets out to create searing, powerful images that audiences will remember. Images make the invisible world of emotions, thoughts, and feelings visible. They *show* us a film's theme, set its style and tone, and create memorable visual metaphors.

If a writer doesn't create images, the director has nothing to work with except characters talking in restaurants, driving through streets, and appearing in nice closeups.

IMAGE AS CONTEXT

Drama is not abstract. Every character exists in a specific world: a specific city, a specific apartment, a specific car, in a specific time and place.

When working with images, a writer's first job is to create a world that rings true. It might be a world of coliseums and gladiator fights and Roman camps and battlefields as in *Gladiator*. It might be the world of Elizabethan England, with its political intrigue as in *Elizabeth*. It may be the world of theater, as in *Shakespeare in Love*.

A script's images need to be specific to the particular film. The battle scenes in *Saving Private Ryan* are remarkably different from the battle scenes in *Black Hawk Down*. The prison scenes in *The Green Mile* have a different feel to them from the prison scenes in *The Shawshank Redemption*. The desert in *Crouching Tiger* is very different from the desert in *The*

English Patient. Criminal investigations take place in quite different worlds in *Fargo, The Fugitive, The Silence of the Lambs, Erin Brockovich,* and *Witness.* The wedding scenes in *Four Weddings and a Funeral* look different from the wedding scene in *The Piano* and *My Big Fat Greek Wedding.* The military world in *A Few Good Men* is different from the one in *A Soldier's Story.* The world of politics is different in *Before the Rain, Indochine, Bulworth, The Killing Fields,* and *Lone Star.* The world of crime looks different in *The Godfather, Goodfellas,* and *Prizzi's Honor, L.A. Confidential, The Verdict, The Crying Game, Unforgiven,* and *Bugsy.*

These differences come from writers using visual details of very specific worlds. These details must be authentic. Audiences are far more sophisticated and more visually literate now than they were even fifteen years ago. Many members of the audience have visited New York and Europe and Africa and India and China, so they often know when something doesn't ring true.

If visual details are off, the audience may have difficulty trusting anything that happens in a film. An audience can feel deceived by a writer, and, as a result, they disconnect from a film, not knowing what to believe and what not to believe.

In my work as a script consultant, I often encounter writers who don't know the worlds of their stories. Their details are inaccurate. If a detail is inaccurate, it can affect both story and character, diminishing or destroying a story's potential impact. I've read scripts in which the description of the Moscow airport sounds exactly like the Los Angeles Airport. (It's not.) I've read scripts in which a detective shoots a gun from such a great distance that it could never hit its target. Or in which a horse kicks its back legs higher than any horse ever could. Some scripts show neat gunshot wounds, even though the caliber of the gun would have blown apart most of the victim's body parts. Some scripts show seemingly smart detectives with no knowledge of how to investigate a crime scene. Sometimes an entire story depends on a visual detail. If a writer gets the detail wrong, there's no way to make the story work.

Creating an authentic context requires research, writing about what you know about. Having grown up in a small town, I know when a depiction of small-town life is not accurate. Having grown up with a mother who was a music teacher, I know when music scenes are not authentic and when they are, as in *The Piano* and *Shine*.

Attention to visual detail is a mark of a great writer. If a writer doesn't know the look of a particular time and place from experience, then research is essential. This might require hanging out in a specific environment, looking for details, asking questions, and just noticing what goes on.

IMAGES THAT MOVE THROUGH A FILM

A writer creates images that visually move a story forward, reinforce its theme, and help define its characters. Sometimes a writer creates images that wind their way throughout an entire script, connecting sometimes disparate scenes. In *Making a Good Script Great*, I discussed how the grain image wove its way through the film *Witness*, symbolizing the corruption that John's violent way of life brought to the non-violent community of the Amish.

In *American Beauty*, roses appear throughout the film, representing Lester's transformation from the uptight world of Carolyn's perfect red roses to the dewy spontaneous roses of youthful exuberance.

In *Rain Man*, the linking car scenes represent the main character's journey of personal transformation.

In *The Lord of the Rings*, the repeated images of the ring keep us connected to its important magical properties.

IMAGE AS CONTRAST

Writer-director Devorah Cutler-Rubenstein has been exploring the meaning of images in her work for some years. She uses a concept of contrasting images, which she offered to share with me for this book.

Imagery is powerful. It makes conscious the unconscious. It's one way we as writers and/or directors can show what is really going on underneath all the words, protected feelings, and social convention. Often, imagery reaches into the secret (or not so secret) places of the soul. In the same way that sound, music, and smell can penetrate, images go "in." We don't even know, when we are seeing them, how they're affecting us. It's almost like an invisible trigger that is done visibly, without our awareness. Audience members should feel the images, as part of the flow of the storytelling.

Images can be used for contrast by juxtaposing conflicting images to create tension, surprise, depth, and to highlight the drama inherent in the theme. For instance, if you're working with a theme of man versus nature, then you can use contrasting images of nature and man in the texture of the story. You can also bring these images into the choice of verbs, metaphors, adverbs, and adjectives you use in the description.

The complexity of simultaneous realities can be shown in contrasting images. The cold steel of a sword sinking into a mossy knoll. The branding of a wild steer. A child's boat floating down a polluted steam. Fish swimming freely in streams and then being fried for dinner.

Images can be used to highlight a confusing truth about a character. A slick attorney can be driving a red Porsche, and the license plate might read "Purr." This image can show both his obsession with power and his more sensitive side that doesn't get expressed. This expresses a duality within the character.

It might even suggest where the character needs or wants to grow. Or the red Porsche could have graffiti spray-painted on the side, to show that the character is giving up his attachment to possessions. The visual details can help show the transformation.

We can see the beauty and light of the jungle contrasted with screams and gunshots and dirt and blood in *The Thin Red Line*. In *The Full Monty,* the joyful and naked exuberance of the men contrasts with the dark and restricted world of the factory town. The life-giving water images in *The English Patient* contrast with the dry desert and the images of burned flesh. These contrasting images resonate with us on an unconscious level, deepening our experience of a film.

CREATING THE VISUAL METAPHOR

A writer must do more than just create visuals that *describe* a specific world. The writer must also create visual metaphors.

A visual metaphor is an image that represents something else and carries an idea. It's an image that resonates with us on many, many different levels. It reaches inside us, and we feel it in our gut. We recognize the meaning of the image because, in some way, we've been there.

Perhaps one of the best known visual metaphors in film is the eating scene in *Tom Jones*. As we watch that scene, we know it's not about eating. It's about sexuality, being rebellious, being a bit naughty. It's about the joy and spontaneity of sex, defying conventions and classism, coming of age, screwing up your life, going after the wrong woman. We could go on and on about what that scene means, but we all could agree that it's not about eating. The thigh, the bones, the drinking all represent sex.

In *The Piano*, when Baines dusts the piano, it's clear that he's not just a good housekeeper. The piano is more than just a piano, it's a representation of the woman he desires to touch, stroke, and caress.

To work well, a visual metaphor has to be carefully chosen. Eating string beans or a nice Caesar salad wouldn't mean the same thing in *Tom Jones*. It had to have bone and gristle and slurping and lots of good flesh to chew on. In *The Piano*, dusting the piano with a dust rag wouldn't mean the same as dusting it with his shirt. Dusting naked presents quite a different metaphor than dusting fully clothed.

Visual metaphors might be drawn from anything. A dead-end street might represent a dead-end life. Mirror images can show a distorted reality. A mirror might represent the theme of illusions and deceptive appearances. Broken glass can represent a broken life. Curtains and windows, as used in *The Last Emperor*, can carry the theme of separation, showing the emperor isolated from the outside world. Blood can be a symbol of life or death. Sunrises and sunsets, perhaps the most overused images, traditionally represent new beginnings, happy endings, all's right with the world, the rustlers are gone, the cattle are mooing, the baby is now all better, and everything is just fine.

Shakespeare often used visual metaphors to help clarify a story's meaning. In his plays, when a soul is tormented, it storms—lightning, thunder, hail, rain. The Greek dramatists often used the image of a storm to show that their heroes were no match for the angry gods. Romances often use weather metaphors to represent the passion of love, as in *Wuthering Heights,* with its visual of wind on the wild moors. *Jane Eyre* is filled with secret rooms and passageways that represent the secret yearnings of a man who has a locked-up secret in the attic. *The Piano* uses a labyrinth of trees to show the complexity of its relationships.

Visual images can also be used for irony. Shakespeare and Sophocles showed us, through *King Lear* and *Oedipus Rex*, that sometimes men see clearly and deeply only after they've been blinded. Sometimes in films we see a character who becomes a more complete person after being disabled or having an amputation or a mastectomy. In *Born on the Fourth of July,* we see a man who has found a more complete identity only after he's lost the use of his legs. In *Magnolia*, Earl Partridge becomes a kinder and more generous person on his deathbed.

A strong visual metaphor in a film can add clarity to all sorts of concepts. In *The Silence of the Lambs*, we see the devouring power of evil, represented by sewing skin, which strips victims of any protection, and by Hannibal Lecter's voracious appetite. In *The Fugitive*, the shots of the maze of the city reinforces the cat-chasing-the-mouse aspect of the story.

Filmmakers, by the very nature of their work, make visual choices all the time. They decide how to express a script's ideas through images. They decide whether to set a story in the open countryside or a frenetic city, in an isolated mountain cabin that shows the solitary nature of a character or on a tropical island where sultry and hot weather show passionate sexuality. They choose how to use space. Will they show space that's limited and blocked off, by concrete buildings or other barriers, because someone has reached the end of the road? If so, are they telling us that the lives of their characters are blocked off? Will they use wide-open spaces, with light, to represent the removal of boundaries and barriers and the clarity of wide vistas?

IMAGE SYSTEMS

In many films that are particularly memorable for their visuals, a writer and director have created an image system, a group of related images that expresses a film's theme. I call an image system a traveling metaphor since it threads its way throughout a film. When an image system works well, it unites a film into a cohesive whole.

Sometimes an image system represents a story's journey. If you want to show a journey of love, you might choose images that show a process of awakening. This might be represented by a progression of dark to light images, or small and claustrophobic spaces to open and expansive spaces or dull colors to bright colors. When we're without love, we may feel dark and a bit blue, and perhaps everything is dim. As we fall in love, we move to hope and light and feeling light-hearted and light-headed and sometimes light on our feet. Things grow with love, so love is sometimes represented by a movement from dead or inert things to growing things.

Seasons are often used to show changes in a character or a theme. The changing seasons in *Driving Miss Daisy* show Daisy's changing attitudes to Hoke, to issues of race, and to her society. The changing seasons of *Dead Poets Society* represents different parts of the boys' lives. The boys begin school in the autumn, with its crisp colors and bracing new beginnings, and death comes in the winter, when the snow represents covering up and silencing the truth.

An image system can show the transformation of a place or a person. During the course of a film, a house might be built, representing the building of a relationship. The growth of a pet can symbolize changes within a character. A plant can grow or die to show a life flourishing or diminishing.

Any group of images that show change can help us understand a character's journey. In *Gone With the Wind*, the changing images of Tara (the O'Hara's family home) tell us about the changing fortunes of Scarlett. They show us that, just like the house, Scarlett suffers, but manages to survive.

Using an image system to define character

Sometimes an image system is used to define a film's characters. If you watch *Fargo*, you'll see an image system that contrasts warm and cold. Warm-hearted Marge is defined by warm images, and the cold-hearted killers are defined by cold images. Notice how the Coen brothers show these contrasts:

The film opens showing Jerry driving through ice and snow to meet the hired killers in a bar. On the way to the kidnapping, the killers drive through snowy Minnesota. After kidnapping Jerry's wife, Carl and Gaear kill several motorists and leave them bleeding in the snow. Later, Carl meets Wade in the snow, kills him, and then buries the money in the snow. The script describes the images:

> He [Carl] slogs through deep snow, down a gulley and up the embankment to a barbed-wire fence. He kneels at one of the fence posts and frantically digs into the snow with his bare hands, throws in the brief-case of money and covers it back up.
>
> He stands and tries to beat the circulation back into his red, frozen hands.
>
> He looks to the right. A regular line of identical fence posts stretches away against unblemished white.
>
> He looks to the left. A rectangular line of identical fence posts stretches away against unblemished white.
>
> He looks at the fence post in front of him.
>
>   CARL
>   Mmmmphh . . .

Contrast this with the script's next description:

> INT. HOTEL ROOM
>
> Marge is sitting on the unmade bed. She is ready to leave, already wearing her parka.

Everything about Marge is warm. We first see her snuggled with her husband under a warm, cozy comforter when the phone rings, telling her about the murder.

Marge goes to the crime scene, dressed in a warm, cozy, down jacket. Lou says, "Margie, thought you might need a little warm-up," as he hands her a cup of steaming coffee.

When Carl watches television, he gets only snow, but in the next scene, Marge watches a television documentary about the beetle that burrows into the warm earth. When Marge captures the killer, she wears warm earmuffs. And, at the end, as Marge looks out over the sky, the earth, the road—all white—she stills sees everything as warm and beautiful and says, "And it's a beautiful day."

Whereas *Fargo* uses an image system of warm versus cold, *The English Patient* uses an image system that contrasts moist and dry. It uses life-giving images of water and shade and anything moist, setting them in opposition to deathly images, represented by desert images that are dry and burnt and withered.

The twelfth-century nun Hildegard von Bingen—a visionary essayist, playwright, and composer—wrote about the contrasting meanings of moisture and dryness: "Moisture and greenness have to do with innocence, love, heart, feelings, and tears. All of the fluids in our body become moist when we are moved—we cry, we lubricate, we bleed—all of the numinous experiences of our bodies have to do with moisture, and it's moisture that brings life to this planet, that is the cure for the desert experience and the cure for aridness." Hildegard said that the major sin of humanity is aridness and its major need is to bring moisture and greenness back into people's lives. Moisture brings healing to those who are dry.

The English Patient is a story about healing—about Hana's healing through the love of Kip, and about the Count's healing as he remembers his love affair with Katharine. Throughout, images of moist and dry show us where and how healing is happening, or not happening.

The first image in *The English Patient* shows a hand, with moist paint, painting images of swimmers in a cave in the middle of the desert. We then see an image of a plane flying across the arid earth. It is shot down and it explodes. The Count has been burned by the crash and explosion. Bedoins from the desert put a moist ungent on his face, and then put a dried mask on top of that, and a moist cloth on top of that. As the Count begins his healing journey, it's late afternoon. Shadows are long, the desert is cool.

Hana takes the Count to a villa to recover from his wounds. The villa has a pond by it and green trees surrounding it. There, Hana feeds the Count a very juicy plum. Later, in flashback, Katharine and the Count begin their relationship when they're caught in a sandstorm. While they wait for the sandstorm to stop, she offers him life-giving water.

There's a lot of washing of hair in this film. Hana washes her hair. Kip washes his hair, and Hana offers him olive oil as a conditioner. Katharine washes the Count's hair with plenty of shampoo and water. We're also shown baths. Katharine loves to bathe. Her husband says she's in love with the plumbing in Cairo. Katharine and the Count take a bath together the morning after they first make love. As Katharine and the Count talk about what they love, she tells him she loves water and hedgehogs.

In one of a film's most magical scenes, Kip takes Hana to see some frescoes high up in a bombed-out church. Here again, we find contrasting moist and dry images. The torch she uses to look at the frescoes has a cool blue flame. The frescoes have been created with moist paint. Hana moves through the air as if she's a swimmer moving through water. As she swings, we hear the plucking of violins, which sound like drops of water.

The day the war ends, it rains. Hana and the others take the English Patient outside to feel the rain, running with his stretcher around the pond.

When Katharine is dying in the desert cave, she talks about how she always wanted an elaborate funeral in her green garden.

WRITING WITH IMAGES

Writers can make their scripts more cinematic by choosing adjectives that help the reader and a potential director visualize a story. Describe specifics. Instead of writing, "The boat is by the shore," try "The little red boat bobs by the stormy shore." Instead of a simple fire, you might have a "consuming fire" or a "devouring flame."

When writing description, think about all your senses. How can you make your script more cinematic by describing a scene's visual, auditory, and tactile elements?

Sometimes the writer and the director are the same person, and the images are created as part of the warp and woof of the entire project. In both *Do the Right Thing*, which was written and directed by Spike Lee, and *The Piano*, written and directed by Jane Campion, we see a creative use of color and light. Spike Lee bathes his whole film about a hot day in Brooklyn in red. In *The Piano*, Jane Campion bathes a number of scenes in blues. Whereas red is the color of passions, heating up to the breaking point, blue is a color that elicits distance and coolness, reinforcing Ada's separation from others.

Well-described images, when not overdone, have the potential to make a story come alive, to define a theme, and to entice a director to eagerly embrace a film. Such images help make a film watchable, enjoyable, entertaining, and memorable.

8

There's More to a Character than Meets the Eye

A writer sets out to create deep, memorable characters. Characters with drive. Characters who yearn and desire. Characters who are passionate about something. Characters who will do almost anything to get what they want. Characters with multiple *layers*.

A multi-layered character is made up of the following four elements: the Who (Who is the character?), the What (What does the character want?), the Why (Why does the character want it?), the How (How does the character get it?).

WHO: What kind of personality does a character have? What are the details of a character that determine how s/he approaches what s/he wants? Is a character shy and reclusive? Mistrusting? Overly sensitive? A happy-go-lucky type? A person who hides the truth? A supportive type who's a good friend?

WHAT: What does the character want, and what is the character willing to do to get it? This is the external character, defined by action.

HOW: How do characters get what they want? How do they fulfill their desires? Procrastinating? Knocking over everyone in their way? Using their powers of persuasion? Negotiating? Acting with determination? Doing intensive research? Becoming emotional? Bonding with others?

WHY: Why is a character driven? Usually a character is driven by a psychological need. It might be an unhappy event in childhood that can only be resolved through actions in the present. It might be a relationship with someone the character loves or hates. It might be someone demanding some action from the character. It might be a fear of authority. Most of the time, at least part of this drive will come from the character's backstory.

Characters are also driven by their values. A desire for justice. A belief that love is the most important quality in the world. A desire for retribution. Compassion. A commitment to nonviolence. A belief that only the fittest survive. A belief that reconciliation is the only way to meet death without regret.

A sympathetic protagonist's value system will always be positive. The antagonists' value system will also be positive, in the antagonist's eyes. Even the worst people don't usually see themselves as evil. They see what they're doing as working toward a good outcome.

How do these four layers work in a script?

WHO?

Personality could be defined as an individual's basic attitude toward life expressed through particular behavioral details. The person might be an extrovert or introvert or a thinker or someone who responds emotionally to stimuli. Yet, even within these categories, there will be vast differences.

If someone is extroverted and vivacious, we expect to see that person relating to other people with interest and curiosity. Such people are easily at home in social situations. They're energetic, with a positive outlook on life. Optimistic extroverts will probably smile and laugh easily and be open and accessible to others. They might be warm, caring, and sensitive.

If you think about the warm extroverts that you know, you will see very detailed differentiations among them. In my circle of extroverts, I find many personality differences.

One person expresses herself very physically. She loves to have fun, and even as a grandmother, she's the type who will be right there on the toboggan, squealing with the grandchildren as they slide down the hill. From childhood, she's always been the first chosen to be on the baseball team and the fastest runner. To her, the objective is rarely as important as the fun in getting there, which has sometimes caused her to accept goals that are not up to her level of ability.

Another extrovert I know is intellectually curious and supports others by sharing the wisdom he's learned, both through his own experience and the vast reading he's done. Sometimes he presumes that everyone else is as interested in knowledge as he is and bores his audience. Other times, he's not grounded in reality, and doesn't catch nuances in people's behavior. He's been duped more than once by real life, because it doesn't always match up with his reading. Yet, his love of people and society doesn't allow him to be a recluse.

Another extrovert I know expresses herself through a sexual and sensual response to life. She's always svelte. Always pretty. Always made up. Always stylish. Sometimes her extroversion takes the form of being a flirt, which has gotten her into trouble with men, leading to a pregnancy before marriage, affairs, and two failed marriages. But her extroversion has been balanced by an ability to reflect on her experiences. She's psychologically astute, supportive, honest, and direct. She's hard-working because she loves to work with people. Her success is a byproduct of her love of people. She achieves her goals as a real estate agent, because she loves matchmaking and using her intuition.

Another person I know is caring, kind, soft, warm-hearted, and feminine. She's super-organized. She wants things to go well, and will communicate and communicate and communicate some more, to make sure things work. Sometimes she gets insecure and frenetic. At other times, she becomes manipulative in her desire to have everything go right.

Watching films, you might have noticed how very rarely we see the diversity of personality that we see in real life. Very few characters that I see in scripts are richly detailed and go beyond simply doing the job of the story. This lack of personality detail may be expected of women characters, since 85% of all feature films are written by men. I've been surprised to find that this is also true of male characters. Characters of both genders are often vaguely written and later defined more by an actor's personality than by the creation of a writer.

Many characters start out as stereotypes and *remain* as stereotypes. Most of the scripts I read, even those written by experienced writers, start out by describing the female character as "late-twenties/early-thirties, sexy, and attractive" or, for males, "late-thirties and ruggedly handsome." At this point, a writer has already painted the characters into a corner.

I sometimes challenge my clients to write character descriptions without wasting time on whether or not the main character is attractive. Of course they are. And, if they weren't attractive before hair and makeup, they will be after. Instead, I ask that my clients imply a certain look, and then tell us specific details that will make the character memorable. These might be details about how characters prepare a steak or the kinds of cars they choose and how they drive them or whether they line-dance or dance salsa or whether they like their martini "shaken, not stirred" or whether they like salad dressing "on the side."

WHAT?

What drives a character through a story? What pulls a character toward a goal? Every major character needs to have a want, a desire, a yearning, an intention, an objective, a need. A goal operates on several different levels. Both the protagonist and antagonist have things that they want and things they they don't want.

The goal in most films is clear: The goal might be to find love (*When Harry Met Sally*); to win an award, finish a task, or accomplish something truly difficult (*Shine, Billy Elliot, Shakespeare in Love*); to get revenge (*Gladiator*); to solve a crime (*Fargo*); to find the truth (*The Truman Show, Erin Brockovich*); to save one's country or workers (*Braveheart, Schindler's List*); to get better working conditions or to better one's life (*Norma Rae, American Beauty*); to get promoted and have an office with a window (*Working Girl*); or even to simply sit by the side of the Mediterranean Sea and drink chardonnay (*Shirley Valentine*).

When a goal works well, the audience can identify with a character's desires. In some way, what the character wants and what the audience members want becomes the same.

In *A Beautiful Mind*, John Nash is introduced as a man who "needs to look through, to the governing dynamics, [to] find a truly original idea. It is the only way I will distinguish myself. It is the only way I will ..."

"Matter" adds Charles.

"Yes," replies Nash.

We, in the audience, can probably identify with Nash's desires. Many of us would also like to find some way to distinguish ourselves, so that we matter and make a difference in the world.

If we look back at the character goals mentioned a few paragraphs above, we can see how they can relate to us, even though we may live in a different period or a different culture. Like Schindler, we'd like to do a good deed, and, if given the chance, we hope that we'd have the courage and moral fiber to save lives. Like Wallace in *Braveheart*, we'd like to protect our land. Like Lester in *American Beauty*, we'd like to figure out the meaning of life. Like General Maximus Decimus Meridus in *Gladiator*, we'd like to get back at someone who did us a terrible wrong. Like Shakespeare, in *Shakespeare in Love*, we'd like to complete our work.

A goal needs to be specific and concrete. At the same time, it can also be a universal, abstract, philosophical idea. Yes, Shakespeare wants to complete a specific play. He also wants to fulfill his talents. Yes, John Nash wants to create a great work. He also wants to contribute to society, to use his brilliant mind, to make a difference, to matter in the world.

However, if a character has *only* an abstract goal, we may have trouble figuring out when the character has achieved it. If one wants freedom, what does freedom look like? If one wants self-fulfillment, how will we know when the character is truly self-fulfilled? If one wants to find the meaning of life, when will we know that the person has found it?

In most scripts, the goal needs to be concrete, so that we can see and know with certainty when it's been accomplished. Justice is a broad universal goal, but it will usually be shown as a specific moment when a bad guy is arrested or found guilty or gets his just desserts. We want a moment when we can see a character achieve something very specific that we can recognize as some sort of self-realization and/or accomplishment.

Characters are pulled through a story by external goals that are expressed as needs. Characters are also pulled through a story by external goals that are expressed as fears of what might happen if they don't get what they want. Is a reputation at stake (*The Fugitive*)? Is someone's life at stake, and if your character doesn't save that person, she won't be able to live with her guilt and her knowledge that she wasn't smart enough, clever enough, or determined enough to have realized that goal (*Silence of the Lambs*)? Is his own life at stake (*Braveheart, Gladiator*)?

What is a character afraid of losing? Perhaps he's afraid of losing his identity because he didn't differentiate himself from the others (*A Beautiful Mind*). Or of losing an important relationship (*You Can Count on Me*).

All of these goals are also related to a character's values. Both the protagonist and the antagonist believe that they hold positive values, even if they're harmful to others. Look at how negative values can be phrased as positives: An antagonist might feel that control is necessary to rein in the evil inclinations of youth. Or that domination is a way of protecting and caring for a wife. Or that torture is a way of getting at the truth that can save many lives. Or that an eye for an eye is the way to create a more just world. All of us believe that our personal value systems will lead to good outcomes—at least for us, and often also for the world. We are motivated by what we see as good, not evil.

The internal goal

A character's external goal is influenced by an internal goal. Characters make choices that are driven by their inner desires.

Characters may not be able to talk about their inner desires, or may not believe that they have the words to express what is pushing at them. But they can feel and sense their internal goals, and they know that they have internal need, that they have to resolve. A character's need to resolve something within himself or herself leads to transformation.

In *American Beauty*, Lester is quite aware of his desires. He's just not talking about them with other people. But the audience knows that he wants out of his old life and into a new one. He's had it with superficiality, dishonesty, and inauthenticity. He's getting older and wants insight, spontaneity, and something truer in his life.

Lester is driven by a universal need—the need to come to terms with one's choices and their consequences. For some people, this internal desire leads to action. Lester recognizes that his choices have led to an inauthentic life. By saying "no" to what he used to say "yes," he begins his journey to reclaim his life. He might be a mystery to everyone else, but his actions are not a mystery to himself.

Exploring a character's internal conscious need works well with character-driven stories, particularly if the audience can understand or empathize with the character's need. Part of the brilliance of *American Beauty* is its ability to make Lester's internal need, an abstraction, become concrete. Even when Lester begins to make bad decisions, his desire for integrity stops him: It stops him from making love to the high school virgin. It stops him from taking out his frustrations on his wife. It stops him from judging the journey of his daughter and the neighbor's son too harshly.

In *A Beautiful Mind*, John Nash begins with the knowledge that he has a problem relating to people. By the film's midpoint, he learns that he also has a mental problem. Overcoming these two problems are his two greatest needs—which are expressed as the need to be with his wife and the need to do his work. He says, "The medication makes me blurry. I can't see...[the solutions]." His desire to see the solution is stronger than his desire to be well or to get rid of his hallucination through medication.

Characters who display an inner need know themselves, but they may not know how to solve their personal problems. They may know they have problems, and want to change, but they haven't found the impetus or the right opportunity. The character knows there's a problem. The audience knows there's a problem. The character has a goal—to resolve a problem—but rarely tells anyone about it.

The invisible need

Sometimes a character's true need is invisible to that character, and may even be hidden from the audience until the end of the story. In this case, only a writer knows about it. Think, for instance, about Michael Dorsey in *Tootsie*. Does he know that he needs to be a less-difficult, more-sensitive person? Probably not. He comes to the realization that his journey has made him a better man for having been a woman only at the film's end. Along the way, he is driven by all sorts of external desires: his need to work, his desire to use his talents, his desire for Julie, his desire to help Jeff mount his play, his desire to preserve his friendship with Sandy. However,

Michael cannot accomplish most of his external goals without changing his basic personality. So his need and desire are both unconscious to him.

When a writer works with an invisible need, s/he is working with subtext—unspoken thoughts and motivations—recognizing that unconscious forces may drive characters. Subtext often involves feelings of regret, guilt, frustration, and shame. These feelings may have festered in a character for years, but have never been reflected upon, listened to, or addressed. For much of the script, these feelings might be unconscious to a character, until that character can no longer ignore them due to the push of events and people that surround him or her. Sometimes this push drives a character to action.

HOW?

Characters get what they want through action. Not every person you may meet in life is an active character. Some people just sit around, shoot the breeze, watch the telly, and take what's given to them. They go along with whatever life has to offer. These characters are not essentially dramatic, so there's no reason to write them into your script.

It's not enough for a character's goal to be clear—a character has to take action to realize that goal. A character must do something, not just talk about it. This means that the desire to reach the goal has to be so powerful that it *pushes* the character into action. If characters are wishy-washy about achieving their desire, we in the audience won't root for them. We'll feel distant so we'll sit back and watch them hang out, rather than lean forward and identify with them, wanting them to get what they want.

The particular way a character carries out the action and confronts obstacles further defines that character.

Characters have to be willing to go through a great deal to get what they want. They train (*Shine, Rocky, Babe*), fight (*The Thin Red Line, L.A. Confidential*), investigate and uncover the truth (*Secrets & Lies, Fargo, Quiz Show, A Few Good Men, A Soldier's Story, The Fugitive*), heal (*Awakenings, Born on the Fourth of July*), and assume power and control (*The Last Emperor, Wall Street, Prizzi's Honor.*)

Just for fun, let's compare *Rocky* and *Babe*. Both title characters are underdogs. (Well, one is a human and the other a pig, but nevertheless, they're not at the top of anyone's heap.) Rocky is driven by his lack of self-confidence and his desire to prove himself and make something of himself. He takes actions to reach his goals: allowing others to influence him, training harder, becoming more determined, knowing that he might just be able to pull this off.

Babe, on the other hand, is not ambitious, but he's much too optimistic to be a loser or to see himself as a loser. He's driven by curiosity and a desire to belong. When Babe has to use mean-spirited or condescending tactics, he can't pull them off. Instead, Babe watches others, experiments with different techniques, takes advice, and finally finds his own way of doing the job that he wants to do. For him, it's not a matter of training and working harder, but of listening to what Maa (the head sheep) tells him and being willing to become more his own sweet self in order to be able to fulfill himself and find his place among the farm animals.

We see different actions leading to similar goals when we compare two detective stories, *The Fugitive* and *Fargo*. Sam Gerard, in *The Fugitive*, spends a certain amount of time just thinking and reflecting on the situation. He asks unexpected questions: He asks Charlie about Richard, "Is he smarter than you?" He acts respectfully toward people he interrogates. He asks politely for their cooperation. And he's all-consumed by his job—any time of the day or night, he'll be there.

Marge, in *Fargo*, is more chatty in some of her interviews. She's persistent, but not tough. And her work is not all-consuming. Whereas Sam Gerard is seen without any intimate relationships, Marge has a husband who loves her and a new baby on the way. We see her in family situations: eating a lot because she's pregnant, snuggling with her husband, watching television. A number of scenes show the support that she and her husband give to each other. He makes breakfast for her when she has to go out to see murdered victims. She encourages him in his painting of ducks. In all aspects of her life, she listens, encourages, draws out people.

WHY?

A character's external goals and personality details are further shaded by motivation. Why does a character want a particular goal? What drives him or her to accomplish the goal? What's in a character's background that makes a character want something so badly that s/he can taste it? How much push and energy does a character have?

Much of this push comes from a character's backstory. Psychologist and script consultant Dr. Rachel Ballon says that much of our psychology is determined by our childhood. She asks many of her writing clients the same questions about their characters that she asks her therapy clients about their lives: "What are the beliefs, fears, drives, desires, and basic needs that make up the internal structure of your life? What current self-defeating behaviors are influenced by the past? Where did these behaviors come from? From the family? Childhood experiences? Repressed memories? Peak experiences? From childhood messages that were accepted as truth and have guided his/her behavior throughout life? Since any individual is the sum of all experiences, conscious or unconscious, the past becomes important to an understanding of how a person is in the present.

A character's push and energy are often motivated by relationships with parents. Sometimes a parent's push can be positive. A character might move toward a goal because of parental encouragement and influence. Other times, a parent's push is negative. A character may move toward a goal because of the parents' overbearing pushiness and control.

We can see parental influence, for good and for ill, in such films as *Shine, Quiz Show, The Piano, Heavenly Creatures, Good Will Hunting, Moonstruck, Rain Man, Elizabeth*, and *Terms of Endearment.*

Sometimes a character's parents want that character to follow conventions. Instead, the character goes in the opposite direction. We can see this pattern in such films as *Titanic, Traffic, Elizabeth, Billy Elliot, Dead Poets Society*, and *The Color Purple.* In a film such as *The Cider House Rules*, it's questionable whether the doctor's influence was positive or negative.

In many films, there will be some mention of the way that a character's backstory motivates that character's desires.

In *A Beautiful Mind*, John Nash says, "My first-grade teacher once said that I got two helpings of brain and half a helping of heart." His lack of heart and his admirable intellect motivated him to turn to the abstract world of mathematics, rather than the more concrete world of relationships—especially since he figured out that "I don't like people much, and they don't much like me."

In *Rain Man*, the autistic brother, Raymond, got three million dollars from his father's will, and Charlie got the rose bushes and the car. Charlie tells his girlfriend Susan the backstory of his father's love of the car.

```
                  CHARLIE
        Tell you one story. Just one.
        Y'know that convertible out front?
        His baby. That and the goddamn
        roses. Car was off-limits to me.
        That's a classic, he'd say. It com-
        mands respect. Not for children.
        Tenth grade. I'm sixteen. And for
        once ...I bring home a report card
        ...and it's all As. So I go to my
        Dad. Can I take the guys out in the
        Buick? Sort of a victory drive. He
        says no. But I go anyway. Steal the
        keys. Sneak it out.
```

SUSAN
Why then? Why that time?

CHARLIE
Because I deserved it. I'd done
something wonderful. In his own
terms. And he wasn't man enough to
do right. So we're on Lakeshore
Drive. Four kids. Four six-packs.
And we get pulled over. He called
in a report of a stolen car. Not
his son took the car without permission. Just stolen.

(beat)

Cook County Jail. Other guys' dads
bail'em out in an hour. He left me
there. Two ...days. Drunks throwing
up. Psychos all over me. Some guy
tries to rape me. Twice. That's the
only time in my life ...I was gut-
scared. Shit-your-pants ...heart-
pounding-right-through-your ribs ...
can't-catch-your-breath scared. The
guy knifed my back. I left home. I
never came back.

Motivation need not just come from a character's backstory. In plenty of great films, we know very little about the main character's backstory, although we might sense it. If we don't know that backstory, it's not unusual for a line of dialogue to articulate where that character's motivation does come from.

In some films, motivation is intrinsic to the character. In *Witness*, we don't know anything about John and Elaine Book's parents, but Elaine lets us know that John has always had integrity. We know that Jane in *Broadcast News* has always been ambitious, both by comments made about her and from a scene at the beginning of a film in which we see her as a bossy child.

Motivations also come from negatives. What is the character's worst fear?

For some, like John Nash in *A Beautiful Mind*, it's failure. For some, it's dying with regrets *(Magnolia)*. For some, it's being found out for the wrongs they've done *(Nixon)*. For Henry Hill, it's no longer being part of the mob *(Goodfellas)*.

A character, however, can't be motivated only by a negative. If there's something a character doesn't want, then there has to be something s/he does want. Otherwise, that character is going to be passive and just hang out in the story, without any energy or push toward a goal. A passive character becomes a static character, rather than a dramatic character who is going somewhere.

If a character is pushed by a negative, s/he will find something to want that is the opposite of that negative. If parents want a daughter to marry someone conventional, the daughter will substitute someone unconventional *(Titanic)*. If parents were lost, abandoned, neglectful, or dead, the character might substitute an intense yearning to belong or to re-connect *(Babe, Field of Dreams, The Color Purple, E.T.)*.

A stand-in for parental figures can be society and culture, which asks characters to be conventional. They then need to find substitutes that help them find their true identities. In some films, this takes a while. In *Good Will Hunting*, Will struggles to find a positive motivation. He has chosen to simply "hang loose" for most of his life, rather than follow either the dictates of his parents or society. He's so out of touch with his own heart, he has no idea what he wants. By the end, he knows he wants Skylar and is willing to take action to get her.

In most cases, it will be clear where a character has turned for a substitute motivation. John Nash turned to the quest for truth: "There is a crystalline architecture to the universe we can only glimpse. That is the only truth. The math of things, the math of everything, the secrets implied by the world in whispers."

Often a character chooses a substitute and then discovers something even more important. Billy Elliot wants his father's love. When he can't get it, he turns to dance. Soon he discovers that freedom and self-fulfillment are as important to him as his father's love. Luckily, by the story's end, he gets both. Erin Brockovich wants a job, but eventually realizes that justice is more important than the paycheck or even her own self-esteem. Truman in *The Truman Show* wants happiness and contentment, but eventually realizes that truth and love are more important.

A character's backstory can include a dysfunctional childhood. This might create a child who always wants to right a wrong or is always distrusting or always wants to get back at adults. Many writers write about of their unhappy childhoods— and sometimes wonder if they'd have anything to say if things hadn't been so bad. A violent background could lead a character to join the police force in order to get rid of violence— forever. And yet, that same character might find that it's difficult to avoid violence to resolve a problem, because that's what's been learned.

A teacher might have been drawn to the profession of books and learning, because she learned to escape her neglectful parents through books. As a result, she finds that she withdraws from people who become too confrontational or demand too much of her. She learns to live in her mind and in the world of ideas.

Characters can be driven by a desire to be like their parents, or unlike them. And they may or may not succeed.

In many cases, the audience never needs to know a character's backstory, but a writer should. Since the backstory drives the psychology of a character, the more a writer knows, the more backstory information can seep into dialogue. A backstory can be implied, and the audience will then *sense* something about what happened in the past. We can guess that a character had a happy or unhappy childhood. We can guess that there have been difficult dynamics within a character's family or with an ex-spouse or with a character's career.

Sometimes, a backstory is talked about in a film, because it's so important that it drives all the character's decisions. In *Moonstruck*, Ronny hasn't talked to his brother Johnny for years, and doesn't intend to come to Johnny's wedding. There's a good reason for this:

```
                    RONNY
          (holds up his left hand to Loretta)

     Look. It's wood. It's fake. Five
     years ago I was engaged to be mar-
     ried. Johnny came in here, he or-
     dered bread from me. I put it in
     the slicer and I talked with him
     and my hand got caught 'cause I
     wasn't paying attention. The slicer
     chewed off my hand. It's funny
     'cause — when my fiancée saw that I
     was maimed, she left me for another
     man ...I lost my hand. I lost my
     bride! Johnny has his hand. Johnny
     has his bride.
```

A happy childhood can also drive actions in the present. We tend to think that all dramatic action comes from dysfunction, but that's not necessarily so. I know that many people didn't have happy childhoods according to psychologists and according to many of my friends and acquaintances. However, I was one of those fortunate people who had a happy childhood, and I've often reflected about how that has driven my own wants and desires. My curiosity was always acknowledged and affirmed by my parents, which taught me to be very curious about people and things. This sometimes drove my teachers to exasperation, but it also enhanced my creativity and my fascination with many things in life, from music to physics to travel to learning about other cultures.

In high school, my little town of Peshtigo, Wisconsin, felt very limiting. This drove me to want to get out, to see, and to live in the big, big world. Since my parents affirmed my desires,

I didn't have to leave my home town out of rebelliousness, but out of a natural desire to grow. This freedom allowed me to stay connected to my roots, and to return now and then, with greater appreciation of my home town.

When creating characters, happiness, support, a good family life, and a loving community can also create dramatically interesting characters. Although we have only a few examples of this, we can see happy, functional, probably-had-a-good-background characters in *To Kill a Mockingbird, The Lord of the Rings, You Can Count on Me, Life Is Beautiful, Saving Private Ryan, Fargo, Avalon, Big,* and *Grand Canyon.*

THE UNDERLYING VALUE SYSTEM

If the story has only an external goal, it can seem derivative or predictable. Something deeper has to be going on than catching the bad guy or winning the contest. To deepen a story, a script has to say something about the human condition. We in the audience need to identify with the larger themes that can motivate a main character—the search for authenticity, the desire for justice, the push toward excellence, the striving for fulfillment.

Depending on your own value system and your own psychology, the starting point for your characters could be positive or negative value systems. Many writers admit that they write from the wrongs done to them as children. They might write from a desire to get back at the world and to show others that they were wronged. They might write from a desire to right the world and make it better for others than it was for them.

In the film *Gladiator,* we might ask if the gladiator's underlying value system demands revenge or justice. Although his actions look as if they're driven by a personal desire to avenge the death of his family, we also see indications that he is driven by a greater value as well. He seems, in Act One, to care about creating a just state, so part of his desire seems to be to right the wrongs of the state that resulted in the good emperor's death and to overcome the evil done by the new emperor.

In *A Beautiful Mind,* John Nash speaks about his desire to solve a great mathematical problem in order to prove that he matters. He is driven by his superior intelligence, which partly manifests itself through his condescending attitude to his peers and teachers, whom he considers beneath him. Yet, on an unconscious level, he seems to strive for things of the heart, not just of the head. He creates, in his mind, a government agent who values his abilities. This is the ultimate proof of his superior intelligence—by unlocking a puzzle, he can save the world. But he also creates a delusional world that contains a friend and a child who are expressions of his heart, not just his head. Eventually, he has to decide whether to continue in his world of illusions or to contribute to society by relating emotionally: to his wife, his child, and his peers.

A story's underlying value system can be focused on individual values, such as the drive toward authenticity, which we find in *American Beauty, Dances with Wolves,* and even *Driving Miss Daisy,* in which Miss Daisy discovers a truer self that is more connected to others who are beyond her social circle. A story's value system can be a social value system—a fight for justice, peace, freedom from oppression, or equality, as we find in *Do the Right Thing, Boyz N the Hood, Thelma & Louise, Erin Brockovich,* and *A Few Good Men.*

HOW DO MULTIPLE CHARACTER LAYERS WORK TOGETHER?

In a great film, the character layers—the who, what, how, why—are connected and push each other. Story decisions are not arbitrary but the product of the characters, the story, and the theme working together as an integrated whole.

In *The Piano,* Ada's *external want* is to get back possession of her piano. And she's willing to do a great deal to get it. *How* does she do it? By allowing a man to demean her while, at the same time, slowly learning to enjoy sensuality and sexuality. *What kind of a person* is she? She has always been objectified by men—first by her father, later by the father of her child. She knows mistreatment, and even expects it. She is used to being owned, possessed, and abused by men, but they can't own her spirit, which finds expression through her piano. She has been deeply wounded by all of the men in her life. She got back at them and at her society by becoming mute. They wanted her to be a silent object, so she has found some power in giving them the ultimate silent woman who can't and won't talk.

Notice that it isn't just music that moves her, but her piano, a specific, concrete object. And, throughout a film, the piano becomes more and more specific: the piano that is out of tune, the piano that needs dusting, the black keys that she wins back, the note that she removes from the piano and sends to Baines. For those of you who play the piano, you may have noticed that she gives away one of the most important notes on the piano—one of its middle keys that is always used in most every piece. This action shows how much she values Baines.

The piano is Ada's object of passion. It defines her identity. The loss of the piano is the loss of almost everything that she cares about. As a result, she keeps to herself, hides, deceives, rebels, and refuses to be owned by her husband. She also goes against her natural desire not to have intimacy, but allows intimacy only in order to get back what is more important to her than any sense of propriety or self-respect.

Although Ada is defined by a metaphor, the piano (which represents her soul, her spirit, and her passion), as she falls in love with Baines, she discovers a deeper value than the piano. She begins to see her soul as bigger than just an instrument. It includes partnership, love, and sexuality. Her new values drive her to free her passion and spirit, which is limited in Act One and Act Two. During Act Three, she learns that her spirit can exist in a larger world. By the story's end, she discovers that she can have her piano, her husband, and even her voice.

The film *The Silence of the Lambs* also uses a metaphor to dimensionalize the main character, Clarice Starling.

Starling wants to find the senator's daughter. That is her external goal. *How* does she do it? Through all the techniques that she's learned as an FBI agent in training: asking questions, following orders, being intuitive, pursuing clues, figuring it out, strategizing, etc. *Why does she do this? What* is her psychology? Her desire to help others was formed by her inability to save the innocent lambs on the farm when she was young. The silence of the lambs, mute witnesses to her inability to save the innocents, is a metaphor that enhances her character by giving her a backstory, a flaw, and an unresolved conflict.

Her overriding value system drives her desire for justice and her desire for a just world in which the innocents aren't killed. Clarice is given further dimensions through her relationship with Hannibal Lecter, who has his own similar underlying values. He also desires justice. He doesn't go after the innocents, but those he considers guilty. Hannibal, of course, uses entirely different means to accomplish his goals. Although we know little about his childhood (perhaps he didn't get enough to eat), we clearly see expressions of his distorted psychology, which is partly formed by his brilliant mind and his ability to be alone.

With all three of the characters I've just discussed—Ada, Clarice, and Hannibal—we can surmise a great deal about their psychologies because what we see *implies* layers of backstory, internal desires, and unconscious motivations. This is an aspect of a rich character—his or her implied layers, which a writer doesn't tell us about directly.

Although nothing in *The Silence of the Lambs* tells us much about Hannibal's backstory, we can sense a consistency about his character that suggests the writer has done his homework and knows his character well. Just through knowing the character of the adult Hannibal, I have no doubt that young Hannibal did not play easily with other kids. I have no doubt that he spent a great deal of his childhood time alone. I presume that he considered himself superior to other children, not just because of his superior intelligence but because of what he considered his superior sense of justice. I expect that Hannibal thought little of the views or values of others. I expect that he pulled a number of wings off flies, and probably performed more than one operation to see what was inside the neighborhood dogs and cats, and how they tasted. What would lead us to these ideas? The scenes of him in solitary, still and seemingly complete. The fact that he became a cannibal, the ultimate socially unacceptable being. The scenes that show he respects justice—by showing what he thinks of Chilton, the police, the senator, and others.

Like any good villain, Hannibal isn't painted entirely evil. He is tempted by the idea of being able to see out a window. I would guess that, as a boy, he played by himself in nature and now misses it. And his willingness to engage in conversation with Clarice shows a respect for her intelligence and some kind of fascination about the truth in her life. As such, he acts as a kind of mentor to her, leading her to face her background and become more open. At the same time, this doesn't mean that his interest in her is innocent and altruistic. He might be finding a kindred spirit who has her own dark places, although quite different from his own.

WHAT CAN GO WRONG WITH A CHARACTER'S DESIRE?

In most films, the main character has a strong desire. In some films, this desire is not clear. Think about the film *Good Will Hunting*. Do you think Will found an alternative to the desires of his parents, society, and teachers? At the film's end, Will turns down a job and leaves for California to be with his girlfriend. But has he really found a substitute desire? At the end, it's unclear whether he found or will find a way to use his considerable gifts. Did you accept this ambiguity or did you want to see a process that showed he had undergone some movement in his transformation?

Imagine an ending with more clarity. Surely a brilliant mathematician can find some way to succeed without compromising himself. And, would Skylar really want an unemployed boyfriend hanging out with her while she does graduate work? What might you, as a writer, have done instead?

Think about the film *Il Postino*. Mario has two desires: to win the love of Beatrice, which he does by the second turning point, and to be a poet, which is suggested now and then throughout the script and seems to have been achieved off-screen by the film's end. Mario's first desire is planted quite early in the story. He watches a newsreel about Pablo Neruda, a poet who writes beautiful love poems. He hears about the love that women have for Neruda, and the love that Neruda has for women. Mario has the same desire for the love of a woman, but he needs a woman. He finds Beatrice. Toward the end of the second act, he and Beatrice come together in spite of the opposition of Beatrice's aunt.

But just as this conflict has begun to build, it suddenly disappears and they get married. By seventy-five minutes into the film, Mario's first desire has been realized.

Mario's other desire—to be a poet—is less clear. It's implied that Mario may want to be a poet because Neruda is a poet, and that he believes that poetry will help him win over Beatrice. So Mario's desire for poetry seems to be a means to an end, rather than an end in itself.

We don't clearly see Mario writing. We see him trying to write poetry once by the window—or, at least, it seems that he's writing poetry. (The scene is unclear.) We see his admiration of Neruda, the poet of love. At the end, we see Mario at a protest rally, where he was asked to read a poem. But we see little action from Mario. We have no way of knowing if Mario really loves poetry or if he really wants to write poetry. Although we're told that he wrote a political poem, most of the film showed that he was more interested in writing and reading love poetry.

As film viewers, we tend to think that all writers' choices are conscious. We presume that if something is unclear, a writer wanted something to be unclear or non-dramatic. But this isn't always true. Sometimes a writer just didn't notice a lack of clarity. Sometimes it's just sloppy writing. Sometimes a writer's decisions reflect the absence of craft.

A script is a combination of conscious and unconscious choices. During the rewrite process, the unconscious processes are usually thought about consciously. If a writer only writes one draft or is only concerned about one aspect of a script, some choices will be arbitrary. Many writers focus each rewrite on a different aspect of the script, doing one rewrite for structure, one for character, and another for dialogue. In this way, the writer can concentrate on a different element in each draft to make sure everything works.

9

Do Your Characters Change and Grow?

Life is about change. If we don't grow, we slow and sometimes come to a dead halt. Without change, we repeat the same patterns. We stop journeying. We no longer transform. Most great drama is about events dramatic enough and traumatic enough to influence characters and to force characters to change.

I define a transformation as a movement toward becoming more fully human and more fully one's own self. We transform as a result of the effects of events and other people. By my definition, our transformations are always positive. They move us toward positive change and growth. We might say that we transform into more dimensional people. We find greater skills and resources within ourselves. We become better people. We learn to respond to life's pressures, and we develop strong personal character as a result.

Sometimes change is negative, and characters regress rather than transform. I call negative change—movement *away* from becoming more fully human and more fully one's self—regression. People encounter problems that they cannot rise above. They become depressed, angry, enraged, out of control. They ruin their lives and the lives of those around them.

Occasionally, a great drama doesn't deal with change at all. It tells it like it is. It shows and describes a situation, perhaps analyzes it, perhaps gives insight into it, but keeps us at a distance from the characters whose lives we watch unfold. In *The Remains of the Day*, the drama comes from Stevens' inability to change when faced with changes in the socio-political climate around him, and the possibility of forming a close relationship.

Some critically and commercially successful films are heroic stories in which a hero is tested and passes the test but does not transform. James Bond and John McClane (*Die Hard*) don't transform. They simply prove their heroism.

In other films, the main character doesn't transform, but others do. In *Driving Miss Daisy*, Hoke doesn't transform, but characters around him do. In *Dead Poets Society*, Keating doesn't transform, but his students do.

Sometimes, several characters transform within a film. In *The Thin Red Line*, Witt changes from a young man who avoids combat, having gone AWOL six times, to a warrior who gives his life to save others. Captain Staros, who led his company for years, was willing to throw it all away when he bucked the colonel and defied orders. Soon after, he backed away from combat and from the military system. And a minor character who pulled gold teeth from the dying Japanese undergoes a change of heart and throws away the gold, weeping with remorse and horror.

WHAT IS TRANSFORMED?

My idea of transformation implies that something is wrong or out of balance or flawed, so it needs to be changed. Greek heroes usually had a fatal flaw that was their downfall because it prevented them from transforming. In our present Western civilization, there may not be a character flaw, but a problem that keeps someone from living a fuller and happier life. Sometimes this problem is defined in psychological terms: a fear of intimacy or of commitment, distrust of others, selfishness, lack of assertiveness for women or too much aggressiveness for men, cowardice, rigidity. Sometimes this problem is an emotional wound that must be healed. Perhaps it's the result of a childhood incident that was never resolved.

Sometimes a character's flaw or problem is ethical or moral: dishonesty, corruption, manipulation, greed, the use of power to oppress others.

A character's problem doesn't need to be a negative. It may be a quality that is usually considered positive, but in a certain situation becomes a problem. For instance, I grew up in a small town in the northwoods of Wisconsin. I was well protected, naïve, innocent, positive, and trusting of the world around me. Nothing was wrong with this set of qualities until I encountered the betrayals and corruptions and insensitivities of the larger world. My positive qualities then became a problem, since they left me unprepared to handle these realities. First, I didn't believe what I was seeing. Then, I felt victimized. Yet, I didn't want to give up my positive attitude toward life. I felt angry, but since we didn't express our emotions in Wisconsin in the 1950s and 1960s, I was in dire need of some sort of transformation. I had to find a way to put wisdom together with innocence, strength together with flexibility, and trust together with discernment.

HOW DOES TRANSFORMATION HAPPEN?

Many times, people exert positive influences on our lives—sometimes as good examples, sometimes through their advice, sometimes through their support and care. However, our transformations occasionally occur because of negative influences. We meet an evil "witch" (in whatever form s/he might take) and surprisingly find that we have the resources to handle this meeting. Our skills for dealing with evil folk might be rusty, undeveloped, or underdeveloped, but in the best cases, our lives' natural transformational journeys strengthen our ability to handle adversity.

Events, both positive and negative, make or break us: Sometimes an actual physical journey transforms us. New vistas, new experiences, new interactions with new places and new cultures bring out strengths that we didn't know we had.

Although the most important life transformations work on both conscious and unconscious levels, film is a visual medium, so transformations have to be *shown*, not just talked about. Therefore, many cinematic transformations are external: Characters learn a skill or overcome a disability or struggle to fulfill a dream. However, since transformation is also an internal process, stories about self-realization, healing, and reconciliation may show characters who become deeper, kinder, more sensitive, more capable of relating to each other.

The external transformation

The simplest transformations are external: A character learns to do something by the end of Act Three that s/he was unable to do in Act One.

Rocky becomes a championship boxer (*Rocky*). Rita becomes educated (*Educating Rita*). Someone may learn to dance (*Billy Elliot*), play piano (*Shine*), run (*Chariots Of Fire*), or simply learn to manage life (*My Left Foot*). Someone may become a wise Queen (*Elizabeth*), succeed at getting audiences to see their act (*The Full Monty*), defeat the enemy (*Braveheart, Ghost, Gladiator*), become more creative (*Dead Poets Society*), build the baseball diamond (*Field of Dreams*), overcome racism (*Mississippi Burning*), overcome injustice (*Norma Rae, Gandhi, Erin Brockovich*), succeed at a job (*Wall Street, Working Girl, Places in the Heart*), catch the bad guy (*Witness, The Verdict*), go from little to big and little again (*Big*), or become a championship sheep dog (*Babe*).

Most of these films show that the underdog triumphs—a theme that can easily become predictable and derivative unless it is deepened with strong and sympathetic characters and an original storyline.

In most films that show external transformations, these outward transformations represent the more important inner transformations of characters.

The internal transformation

An internal transformation is a character's movement from a negative personal trait to a positive one. If you look at some of the themes mentioned in Chapter 5, you will see many examples of internal transformation in films in which characters resolve life issues and become more capable people by the end of the film.

In movies about children, a child's or teenager's internal transformation often moves from low self-esteem to high self-esteem or from lack of confidence to assertiveness and self-assuredness: *Home Alone, The Karate Kid, Dead Poets Society, Spy Kids, Billy Elliot, Almost Famous, Toy Story.*

Films that revolve around characters in their twenties or thirties will often show internal transformations from personal failure or work problems to success and achievement. Sometimes characters also find love and intimacy in the process: *Rocky, Working Girl, The Full Monty, Jerry Maguire, Shine, Bugsy, Shakespeare in Love.*

Films about characters in their thirties through fifties might show an internal transformation to a new value system, which deepens or humanizes characters, or leads them to greater sensitivity. Sometimes a character's lack of success in the world's terms leads to a different kind of success. Instead of money, fame, and power, a character might find integrity (*Quiz Show, The Insider, Lone Star*) or courage in the face of overpowering obstacles (*Apollo 13, Braveheart*) or justice (*Running on Empty, Silkwood, In the Name of the Father, A Soldier's Story*). Sometimes a character finds success by breaking away from family or culture, discovering a new set of values in the process (*The Cider House Rules, A Room with a View*).

Films about people in their sixties and up often show an internal transformation to reconciliation and resolution (*Driving Miss Daisy, Tender Mercies, Trip to Bountiful*) or realization of what's important in life. In *Melvin's Room, One True Thing, Magnolia*—all of which deal with dying and death—the story shifts from an ill person to a person who is not ill but needs to find deeper values and understand what's really important in life.

Not all internal transformations are dramatic or momentous. Occasionally a film shows a small internal transformation—a character changes his mind. In *The Fugitive*, Sam Gerard changes his mind about Kimble through a series of small story beats that make him increasingly aware of Kimble's possible innocence. In *Driving Miss Daisy*, Daisy changes her attitude toward Hoke, first seeing him as an employee who is always in her way, then seeing him as her best friend. In *Traffic*, Javier changes his attitude toward the law-enforcement system as he sees more of its corruption. In *Chocolate*, the mayor changes his mind about the chocolate woman who has brought so much magic to his town.

WHO TRANSFORMS?

In most films, the protagonist transforms. But not always. Sometimes a supporting character transforms as a result of a relationship with the protagonist. In *Philadelphia*, Andrew goes through a external transformation but very little in the way of an internal transformation. Yet he acts as a catalyst character for the transformations of his lawyer, some of his family, and some of the others in his firm. Keating, in *Dead Poets Society*, is a catalyst for the transformation of most of the boys in his classroom. He doesn't need to change. The boys do. The boys move from conformity to creativity and, at least with Todd, from lack of confidence to the ability to be assertive, expressive, and more spontaneous. In *Chariots of Fire*, Eric Liddell doesn't transform, but those around him are affected by his integrity. In *Unforgiven*, William Munny only marginally transforms, since he has already given up his old life by the time the story begins. But the journey he takes with the Schofield Kid transforms the Schofield Kid, so that he won't become the kind of person that Munny has been. In *The Mission*, Mendoza begins as a warrior, but changes as a result of his relationship with the priest.

STRUCTURING THE TRANSFORMATIONAL ARC

Generally, a transformation, like a subplot, needs a minimum of three beats: the problem, the realization, the change. However, few transformations happen in only three beats—most take ten, twenty, thirty beats or more, reflecting how our real-life transformations take place over a long period of time. Most transformational stories will need a full two hours and all three acts to set up, develop, and prove a character's transformation.

Most transformational storylines can be graphed out with the same structure as major plotlines, with a catalyst, turning points, sometimes a midpoint, and a climax.

Act One sets up a character's problem that needs to be resolved if that person is to gain happiness, fulfillment, and/or a strong relationship. The problem might be a mental problem, a character flaw, unresolved family problems, resistances to success or achievement, fear of intimacy, or many other things.

Somewhere within Act One is a catalyst that starts the protagonist's journey. The catalyst is often a negative: such as an accident, an illness, a separation from a parent or a child or spouse, the death of a child, or a failure that forces the protagonist to deal with the problem set up earlier and, in the process, transform.

Sometimes a catalyst is positive: a new girl in town, a new teacher, a promotion, a vacation, or an opportunity to have the adventure of a lifetime.

In most cases, the catalyst of the transformational arc will occur within a story's setup. If a character doesn't begin a transformational journey within the setup, s/he usually does so by the first turning point. In *Dead Poets Society*, Keating teaches his first class thirteen minutes into a film. His teaching style shows that he's a different kind of teacher, a catalyst for the boys' emerging creativity. In *The Silence of the Lambs,* Clarice Starling gets the assignment that will change her life right after the opening credits, and she meets Hannibal Lector about fifteen minutes into the film. In *Working Girl,* Tess discovers her boss's betrayal before the first turning point.

At the first turning point of a transformational arc, characters usually make a choice that will bring them into a situation that will affect them, whether they expect it to or not. Will, in *Good Will Hunting*, doesn't realize that making a deal with the math teacher will change the course of his life. Todd doesn't realize that his decision to join the Dead Poets Society will resolve many of his identity issues. Belle, in *Beauty and the Beast,* doesn't realize that her decision to stay at the Beast's castle will lead to love and redemption.

During Act Two, characters work hard, struggle, try to overcome obstacles, get upset, cling to old patterns, don't get it—all the while continuing to be pushed forward by the people and events of the story.

Then, by the film's midpoint, we begin to see changes in the character. The character has begun to live life differently and new behaviors emerge. At the midpoint of *Jerry Maguire*, *Beauty and the Beast*, and *Good Will Hunting*, all three of the protagonists have a scene that shows them as more loving, more intimate, and more compassionate than they were in the first half of the film.

At the second turning point, characters often have to make decisions—will they stick with their emerging transformations or will they go backward? By the second turning point in *Schindler's List*, Schindler has achieved his goal of wealth. But the transformation he's gone through for most of the film is now tested. He has to decide whether he'll leave with the money or stay to save his workers. He proves his transformation, by staying. Act Three proves the character's transformation, often through one last test that shows that s/he is now open enough to fall in love, confident enough to get the promotion, or strong enough to win the contest.

In some cases, the character announces his transformation. Schindler tells his workers that he could have done more. Jerry Maguire confesses his love to his wife, Dorothy.

In other films, characters show us their transformations, proving that they are different at the end than they were at the beginning (*Elizabeth, As Good As It Gets, Babe, Shakespeare in Love, Jerry Maguire, The Full Monty, Quiz Show, The Piano, Schindler's List*).

In very rare instances, a transformational arc begins at a film's midpoint. In *Secrets & Lies*, Hortense contacts her birth mother halfway through a film. As a result, Cynthia immediately begins a transformation. In the next scene, she begins to be more attentive to her daughter, Roxanne, and buys her steak for a special dinner. Cynthia's change begins to make a change in Roxanne. Roxanne, who has probably not smiled in years, begins to smile, and by Act Three, she actually laughs. Cynthia's and Roxanne's transformations lead to other transformations. In Act Three, Cynthia and her brother, Maurice, confront Maurice's wife, Monica. This confrontation forces Monica and Maurice to tell the truth, which leads to a reconciliation between Cynthia and Monica as well as a reconciliation with the entire family.

It's unusual to begin a transformation this late in a story. *Secrets & Lies* is the only film that I can think of that does this and gets away with it. This late transformation forced *Secret & Lies* to create a tremendous amount of dense, intense, emotional information in Act Three, and forced the story to be played as parallel journeys for half of a film. Act Three was long—thirty-five minutes—but writer-director Mike Leigh and his brilliant actors managed to keep emotional intensity building throughout the act.

You might want to re-watch this film and imagine beginning the transformation at a late first turning point rather than the midpoint. What would you gain? What would you lose? Did you find the first half slow? Or did it hold your attention and feel as if its slow unraveling was much like the way these things unravel in life?

Somewhere in Act Three, the character has to prove his or her transformation. Although this is best done through an action or event, in *Pulp Fiction*, Jules proves his transformation through what he *doesn't* do. When he gets caught in a robbery, he doesn't kill the robbers, which would have been his usual modus operandi. Jules explains his transformation as moving from an avenger to a shepherd.

Two of the best—and best-structured—transformational films are *Tootsie* and *As Good As It Gets*. Although some films accomplish a transformation in ten or twenty beats, these contain thirty to forty transformational beats, and each proves that the character has made a change by the end of Act Three.

Transforming Michael Dorsey

Act One of *Tootsie* establishes several of Michael's qualities: He's a good actor. He's a good friend of Sandy's but has trouble forming intimate, romantic relationships with other women. He's well-liked by his roommate. He's a well-respected acting teacher. And, one more quality is set up at the beginning—Michael is difficult. He's intractable and demanding and thinks he's always right.

In one of the film's early sequences, Sandy asks Michael's help to prepare for a soap opera try-out. Michael is willing to help, and chides Sandy for not expressing her anger. Sandy admits that she has trouble with anger. That's her problem, which is established in Act One, begins to be transformed in Act Two, and is resolved in Act Three.

When Michael accompanies Sandy to the reading, he discovers that his agent did not send him up for a part in a play. When he realizes that no one will hire him because he's too difficult, this information pushes him to make a new decision at the first turning point—to become Dorothy Michaels, who might have a chance of getting hired. Michael would have no way of knowing that putting on a woman's dress would cause so many changes in his life. But when he does, he notices life is different as a woman. This leads to his increased sensitivity to Sandy and Julie (and even to women in the soap opera's television audience).

In Act Two, Michael notices that getting a taxi as a woman is difficult. He begins to be more diplomatic and realizes it's a more effective way to get what he wants. He notices that Ron, the director, is two-timing Julie. And he feels badly for her because of this deception. He wonders why Julie is with such a cad. He begins to notice that Julie has low self-esteem. He notices how Julie allows Ron to walk all over her. And he notices that she drinks too much. This leads to his increased care and empathy for Julie.

Michael becomes more responsive to Sandy's feelings. When he forgets his dinner with Sandy, he realizes that she, too, allows men to walk all over her. He brings her ice cream as an apology, and tells her, "You should be furious with me!" This beat acts as the first turning point of Sandy's transformational arc, and during Act Two, she'll begin to get more in touch with her anger.

Michael works as a catalyst for Sandy's transformation, and Sandy acts as a catalyst for Michael's transformation. Early in Act Two, she gives Michael her opinion of Dorothy, leading him to seeing his role differently.

> SANDY
> You were so terrific about the au-
> dition for the soap - the stupid
> soap! By the way, did you see the
> cow they hired?

> MICHAEL
> Cow?

> SANDY
> I guess they went another way.
> She's just awful.

> MICHAEL
> I heard she was pretty good.

> SANDY
> Baloney! She's supposed to be the
> head of the hospital. Remember how

> you said she's supposed to be a
> tough woman? She's not tough. She's
> a wimp!

MICHAEL
> Maybe it's the lines ... After all,
> she doesn't make up her lines ...

SANDY
> Well, maybe she should. They
> couldn't be any worse.

CUT TO:

INT. STUDIO —

Dorothy and "patient" taping. The female
patient is in an arm cast, sobbing.

PATIENT
> I can't move out, Miss Kimberly. I
> have nowhere to go. I don't know
> what to do.

Dorothy looks at the teleprompter. The
teleprompter shows Dorothy's lines: "Your
husband's problem is that he feels worth-
less without a job. You must try and understand that. Perhaps you should get some
therapy."

INT. CONTROL ROOM —
ALL watching monitor.

DOROTHY
(suddenly)
> Don't lie there cringing ...

Since Michael has begun to see how women allow men to
control them and manipulate them, and how women can be
wimps, he applies what he's learned and begins to make Emily
Kimberly, the character that Dorothy plays, a more assertive

women. He begins changing her lines and helps Julie become more assertive in her role as the nurse.

This has a transforming influence on the women in the soap opera's television audience. They feel empowered by Emily, who becomes one of the most popular soap-opera stars. This leads to a midpoint montage that shows Dorothy's new fame and popularity. She's on the cover of a number of the top magazines. It seems that everyone is watching the soap.

If we look at the journey Michael takes from the first turning point to the midpoint, we can see that he's learning his role as Dorothy. He figures out that she's smarter than he is. She's more diplomatic, so he figures out how to get what he wants without being difficult. He figures out how to make her a stronger person. The end of this arc is the montage that shows Dorothy's success.

In many films, the second half of Act Two is trouble, trouble, trouble. Just as everything looks as if it's going well, everything begins to go wrong. Things become more complicated. The character is caught in an unexpected problem. Michael/Dorothy has gone so far down the road by the film's midpoint that there's no turning back. The character's change is not complete, but it's far enough along that the character can no longer go on as before.

Michael now has two problems: He wants the success he's achieved, and he also wants Julie. He first tries to resolve this by trying to make his dual life as both Dorothy and Michael work. He wants Dorothy to reach her full potential, so he asks his agent to put Dorothy up for some other roles, such as Lady Macbeth.

```
                  MICHAEL
       I feel like I have something mean-
       ingful to say to women ... I've
       been an unemployed actor for years.
       I know what it's like to feel op-
       pressed ... If I could impart ...
       that information, that experience
       onto other women like me —
```

                         AGENT
          There are no other women like you.

At the same time, he tries, as Michael, to start a relationship with Julie, but when he tries to pick her up, she throws
her drink in his face. Clearly Julie isn't interested in Michael,
even though she wants to be friends with Dorothy.

Julie's relationship with Dorothy leads Julie to become more
assertive in her role. She becomes stronger and gives credit to
her coach, Dorothy. Ron realizes that Dorothy has been giving
Julie assertiveness training, which begins to threaten him and
makes him put down Julie. Seeing this, Dorothy confronts Ron,
speaking up to him in a way that Julie is not yet capable of
doing. The lines are an affirmation of Dorothy's identity but
also an affirmation of Julie's emerging assertiveness.

                        DOROTHY
          My name is Dorothy. Not *"Tootsie,"*
          not "Toots," not "Honey," not
          "Sweetie," not "Doll."

                          RON
          Oh, Christ.

                        DOROTHY
          No, just Dorothy. John is always
          John, Rick is always Rick, Mel is
          always Mel. I'd like to be Dorothy.

     She stomps off to an adjoining set. Julie
     looks at Ron for a moment, then moves off
     after Dorothy.

At the end of Act Two, Dorothy goes with Julie to the
farm for Thanksgiving and we see how much Michael has
changed. Instead of ignoring children, Michael/Dorothy holds
Julie's baby close to him. Instead of seeing women as sexual
objects or "just friends," he empathizes with Julie and sees
that tenderness is a big part of love.

By the second turning point, Michael encounters a series of tests that force him to choose between success or love. Of course, since this is a comedy, each test is humorous. Michael/Dorothy tries to tell Julie who he really is, but she misunderstands and thinks that Dorothy is a lesbian and decides they shouldn't see each other. Les, Julie's father, proposes to Dorothy. Brewster tries to seduce Dorothy. Sandy hears that there's another woman in Michael's life. She's enraged, and finally in touch with her anger. Michael wants to unmask immediately, but his agent tells him that if he unmasks now, they'll face a scandal and be sued.

Finally, Michael finds his unmasking opportunity when they have to redo a section of the soap opera—this time live. He unmasks and clarifies that he has become a better man for having been a woman: "Being a woman was the best part of my manhood, the best part of myself."

Tootsie is a film with more subplots than most. There's the Michael/Julie subplot, the Michael/Dorothy subplot, the Michael/Sandy subplot, the Dorothy/Les subplot, the Dorothy/Brewster subplot, the Julie/Ron subplot, and Jeff's play. Each person, each event, and each subplot forces Michael further into his transformation. It takes many people and many subplots to transform Michael because he's a difficult case.

As Good As It Gets

In *As Good As It Gets,* Melvin is introduced as one of the most insensitive, uncaring, mean-spirited, rude people that anyone could ever meet. He's shown to hate dogs, which proves what a terrible person he is. He hates homosexuals. He hates his neighbors. And they hate him. He's racist and sexist. And he has an obsessive/compulsive disorder.

Carol, a waitress, is the only person who seems able to deal with him. She's a woman who doesn't take any guff. When Melvin insults a customer at the restaurant and says they're all going to die, including her son, she makes him swear that he'll never mention her son again. This hits a nerve with Melvin. The next time he comes to the restaurant, she ignores him, but he then asks her what's wrong with her son. She tells him about her son's illness.

Melvin's increased sensitivity makes Carol more sensitive to his potential humanity, and her response to him makes him more responsive to Simon, his neighbor. At the first turning point, when Simon, who is an artist and a homosexual, is beaten up, Melvin is told to take care of Simon's dog. In the beginning of the second act, the dog begins to transform Melvin, which leads Carol to being kinder to Melvin. She tells him that the next time he comes to the restaurant with the dog, he can bring the dog inside. They talk some more. Her kindness to him makes him kinder to the dog. He gets bacon for the dog, takes him for a walk, and allows him to sit beside him as he finishes his book.

The dog has begun to transform Melvin. When he has to give the dog back, he starts to cry. The fact that he is now without a dog forces Melvin to return to his psychiatrist and ask for help.

When Melvin doesn't find Carol at the restaurant one day, he insults everyone. He wants only Carol to wait on him. Desperate to have Carol back in his life, he bribes the busboy for her address. He goes to confront her.

She clearly is not happy to see him, and explains that her son, Spence, is sick. As Melvin is ready to leave, Spence's fever gets worse, so she asks Melvin to give them a lift in the cab. He does. Seeing Spence sick makes Melvin more compassionate. He sends a doctor to take care of Spence and diagnose his condition. Melvin will pay for everything. The doctor promises that Spence will now start to feel a lot better.

Melvin's response to Carol's son makes Melvin more sensitive to others. He offers to take Simon's dog for a walk. And, when Simon tells Melvin that he will lose his apartment because he was beaten up and is unable to continue his painting, Melvin feels sorry for him and sits down to talk with him.

At the film's midpoint, Melvin begins to manifest his humanity. He pays for Spence's treatment, endearing him to the people around him and to the film's audience. Melvin helps Simon.

Carol is confused by Melvin's sudden humanity, so she confronts him. Why is he paying her son's medical bills? Here, at a film's midpoint, Melvin's motive for helping Spence is by no means altruistic. He is doing it mainly to get Carol back to work so that he can go back to his same routine at the restaurant. Yet, he is slowly beginning to be humanized by his associations with Carol, Spence, Simon, and the dog.

In the second half of Act Two, Carol writes a thank-you letter to Melvin. When she tries to give it to him, he won't take it. He insists, instead, that she accompany him and Simon to Baltimore to see Simon's folks, hoping they'll help Simon out. Carol is happy to be on this journey and tells Melvin, "I'm happy and you're my date." They go out to dinner. Melvin insults her, so Carol prepares to leave. She tells him, "Pay me a compliment." He tells her that he has gone back to his psychiatrist and is now back on his medication. He tells her that she makes him want to be a better man. He tells her that she makes him want to take his medicine. Carol asks why he brought her with them. Melvin tells her that he hoped that she'd sleep with Simon so he'd stop being homosexual. She's insulted and leaves, and bonds with Simon. Carol's understanding of Simon helps him draw again. He decides to draw her, and the two spend most of the night talking while he draws.

At the second turning point, Carol tells Melvin that he makes her feel bad about herself. She leaves him. This forces Melvin to look at himself and the consequences of his behavior. He clearly is not getting what he wants out of life: He has no Carol, no friends. He now has to make a choice—to continue his transformation or to return to the isolated life he led in Act One.

His insight into his own sorry plight makes him more caring toward Simon. He invites Simon to stay at his apartment. Simon thanks him and says he loves him. Melvin replies that he'd be the luckiest guy in the world if that did it for him.

Carol returns home and sees that Spence is doing well. She calls Melvin to apologize to him. She tells him that she enjoys his company, but there are problems. Simon encourages Melvin to go over to Carol's. Melvin and Carol go for a very early morning walk. He compliments her. He kisses her and they head for the bakery for breakfast.

Throughout this film, one character's kindness pushes another character toward kindness to others. The characters are catalysts for each other. Frank, Simon, Carol, Melvin, Carol's mother, and the dog all influence each other's transformations.

CREATING A TRANSFORMATION IN A SINGLE SCENE

Most character transformations take place over a long period of time. Occasionally, a transformation can be sudden. Sometimes a film shows us these quick transformations that can take place over a few minutes, an evening, or a few days. In *A Christmas Carol*, Scrooge is transformed overnight, although it takes the entire film to show it.

Around the second turning point of *Pulp Fiction*, Jules and Vincent are almost killed. All six shots fired at them miss them, which Jules considers a miracle. In this one scene, he instantly decides to change his life and tell Marsellus that he's through working for him.

In *Dead Poets Society*, Todd goes through a transformation in class. The class has been asked to write a poem by Monday. Todd works on it throughout the weekend, but in class on Monday, he tells Keating, "I didn't do it. I didn't write a poem." Keating knows that Todd has low self-esteem. He asks Todd to come to the front of the class and give a barbaric Yawp. Todd gives weak, wimpy Yawps, but, prodded by Keating, finds the barbarian within himself. Then, Keating asks him to make up a poem about "Uncle Walt," Walt Whitman, the poet whose portrait hangs in the class.

Todd makes up a poem that is not only imaginative, but shows his low self-esteem and his despairing attitude toward the hopeful possibilities in life.

```
                        TODD
A sweaty-toothed madman ...
I,I close my eyes.
His image floats beside me.
A sweaty-toothed madman,
With a stare that pounds my brain.
His hands reach out and choke me,
All the time he mumbles slowly,
Truth,
Truth is like a blanket that always
leaves your feet cold.
Stretch it, pull it, it will never
cover any of us.
Kick at it, beat at it,
it will never be enough.
From the moment we enter crying to
the moment we leave dying,
it will cover just your head as you
wail and cry and scream!
```

Keating, recognizing Todd's talent and transformation in this one short scene, tells him, "Don't you forget this!"

In *Schindler's List,* Schindler goes through a one-scene transformation. Itzhak Stern tells Schindler that a man is waiting to see him. This man wants to thank Schindler for saving his life. Itzhak brings in a one-armed machinist, who thanks Schindler profusely, to Schindler's great embarrassment. He tells Schindler, "You are a good man. Bless you." Schindler leaves, telling Stern, "Don't ever do that again." Shortly afterward, the one-armed man is shot. Schindler complains to the commandant, who replies: "To believe that a one-armed man can help Third Reich economics." Schindler takes the side of the one-armed man, showing his change in attitude toward him. "He was a metal-press operator, quite skilled."

Fast transformations still need preparation. We believe the transformations in *Dead Poets Society* and in *Schindler's List* because we've seen earlier evidence in these films that these characters were beginning to transform.

In the film *Billy Elliott*, Billy's father transforms in one scene, but his transformation seems to come out of nowhere. Suddenly, he's supportive of his son's dancing. We have to presume that, off-screen, something happened to him: Perhaps he reflected on his son's love of dance. Maybe he realized how much he loved his son. Maybe he felt that he had been too hard on Billy. Maybe someone talked to him and told him to change his attitude. Maybe he noticed a change in his son, which caused him to soften toward him. Something *must* have happened. But we never *saw* the moment of transformation. We never knew where it came from, how long it took to get there, and what events and influences made the father transform. Although this film is charming and wonderful in so many ways, the father's transformation was one of its few problematical parts.

Billy's transformation, however, was believable. We clearly saw the transformational beats: The Need, The Decision, The Struggle, The Triumph.

Billy's father's transformation only had one beat—suddenly it was there. To create a transformation arc for a character, you may want to first think about one of your own transformations. Why did you need to transform? How many people did it take to change you? How long did it take? What made it possible to transform at that time in your life but not before? Did you backslide? How did you and others know that you had changed? After your transformation, did you look and act differently? How?

THOSE WHO CAN'T TRANSFORM

Not all transformations go according to plan. Sometimes a character tries to transform, but can't. In *Goodfellas*, Henry

Hill is too much in love with the mob to make any changes—no matter what pressures exist.

In *Schindler's List*, Goeth tries to transform, but can't. Schindler explains to him that the really powerful person is the one who shows mercy. Goeth decides to try it for a day. He doesn't shoot the young boy who left a smudge on his saddle. He doesn't shoot the woman walking through the camp. He forgives his maid. He practices saying, "I forgive you" to see how it feels. At the end of the day, goodness is too much for Goeth, so he shoots the boy dead.

In *Dangerous Liaisons*, Valmont also has a struggle with his transformation. He's been manipulative and cruel for far too long, so he hardly knows what to do when he starts to fall in love.

In Act One, Marquise de Merteuil challenges him to seduce Cécile. He considers this challenge far too easy. (He has his reputation to think of!) So he makes a deal that he'll seduce Cécile, but he also wants to seduce someone who is much more virtuous and would really present a challenge. At the first turning point, he sets out to seduce Madame de Tourvel.

In Act Two, he manipulates Madame de Tourvel, accuses her of being unkind, and plays into all of her virtuous, kind, naïve, and caring tendencies. She is no match for him. As she starts to fall in love with the seductive and corrupt Valmont, to his surprise, he suddenly falls in love with her. In Act Three, he learns that it's difficult to transform. No resources or influences have prepared him for the love of a good woman. His only confidante is Marquise de Merteuil, who lives her life by cruelty and manipulation.

Because Valmont has been pretending to be transformed by the love of Madame de Tourvel throughout Act Two, only to suddenly find himself truly in love with her in Act Three, he has no idea how to handle love. He's spent his life manipulating, seducing, and throwing away people. He's never cared, valued, or appreciated anyone before. In his world, everything has been a game.

During Act Three, Valmont moves back and forth between sensitivity and cruelty, vulnerability and hard-heartedness. At the end, he achieves a partial transformation, shown by his ability to proclaim his love, but only at his death.

MISSED POTENTIAL TRANSFORMATIONS

Some films imply transformations but never carry them out. In the early drafts of *Witness*, John went through a transformation as a result of being part of the quiet, harmonious Amish farm. Short scenes showed him looking out over the beautiful farm, seemingly yearning for this simpler life. In one scene, he walks through the grain, looking out over the land. These several scenes were reduced to one scene of him looking out the window, plus one line of dialogue: "If I made love to you last night, I'd have to stay, or you'd have to go."

Yet, transformation seems implicit in John's move from his life as a police detective in Philadelphia to a a man forced to hide out on an Amish farm. Wouldn't the simple Amish life affect most people in one way or another? Although John seems more relaxed in Act Three than in Act One, a film has no clear transformational beats that show a transformational arc.

A similar missed opportunity exists in *The Fugitive*. We might ask, "What happens when a doctor, at the top of his profession, is convicted of murder, separated from his wife and friends, has to steal to get money, and is forced to move to an ugly apartment and disguise himself as a janitor?" That turn of events certainly would affect most people. But we never see a transformation in Richard Kimble. He seems to stay the same, regardless of his circumstances.

We might wonder whether this was the fault of the writer, the director, or the actor. If the writer doesn't write a transformation into a script, the director can't direct it and an actor can't act it.

Hundreds of films imply a transformation but don't carry it through. We might ask: Wouldn't a gladiator who lost his wife and his standing as a military officer be changed as a result of these experiences? And, if so, how would he be changed? Who, or what, would be the catalyst for this change? What might he become as a result of his experience?

Would Erin Brockovich be changed as a result of having to live up to the responsibility and assertiveness necessary to right a wrong? What about Andy Dufresne in *The Shawshank Redemption*? He showed us that he could hold his own in prison, but was he transformed? If not, why not? In *Fatal Attraction*, Dan was sorry for his actions, or perhaps simply sorry that they were found out. But did he really change? The ending of *Crouching Tiger, Hidden Dragon* was somewhat confusing: Did the young girl actually transform? In *Terms of Endearment*, did the astronaut transform or simply become a bit more responsive?

WHY ARE TRANSFORMATIONS SO RARE AND SO HARD TO PULL OFF?

If transformations are a normal part of growth and maturity, why don't we find them in more films?

I don't believe that people transform without the influence of other people. Maybe a few desert fathers, meditating in isolated caves, managed to transform by themselves, but most people need the influence of others to change. Since drama is implicitly relational, transformation is a natural process to show in film. But to do so requires that characters be developed dimensionally enough to have the qualities needed to transform each other. They must be both willing and able to exert influence on one another.

This doesn't mean populating a script with talky characters who give advice. Instead, you need to create characters and events that are dramatic enough to force transformations. Simon's beating in *As Good As It Gets* is dramatic enough to start the transformation of Simon and Melvin. The court political intrigue in *Elizabeth* is dramatic enough and threatening enough that either Elizabeth will fail or transform. She has no other choice. When Lester's boss in *American Beauty* fires him, his action pushes Lester into transformation. Earl's declining health in *Magnolia* forces other characters to come to terms with him, which forces their transformation.

The beginnings of transformations can be subtle. A glance between characters and an emotional response can show the beginning of a transformation. When Julie, in *Tootsie,* gives a particularly good performance that wins the applause of everyone but Ron, Dorothy's reaction to Julie's work, Julie's gratitude for Dorothy's help, and Ron's put-down of Julie are shown through glances and a line or two. But they are sufficient motivations for character changes.

Sometimes writers don't create great transformational arcs because they don't observe their own transformations and the transformations of others, so they don't know what transformations look like. Sometimes writers don't understand that actors have a rich emotional vocabulary for communicating inner character changes. A good actor can express thinking, reflection, and realization through facial expressions or changes in posture. It is sometimes said that acting is reacting, and good actors know how to express their inner reactions to the actions of others.

Dialogue delivery can also help to reveal these moments of reflection. Sometimes a writer adds the word "beat" to a line of dialogue to show that s/he wants the actor to pause before delivering the rest of the line.

Just as a transformation is brought about by the influence, advice, and actions of others, once characters undergo transformations, we need to see how they affect the character's world differently, and how others react differently to them. This *proves* a transformation and is usually found at the end of Act Three.

At the end of *Elizabeth*, the Queen has chosen how to rule. This is shown through the way she deals with people who were manipulating and betraying her in the past. Melvin, in *As Good As It Gets*, becomes almost likeable by the film's end, and others are willing to relate to him. And Michael, in *Tootsie*, finally gets the girl.

A transformation gives a writer an opportunity to express personal belief systems and viewpoints about humanity. Sometimes this sort of message is expressed through action. Often it's also expressed through dialogue.

10

Say It Well

I f done well, a film's dialogue is memorable. We quote it, and sometimes live by it. It crops up in our common language. We have film dialogue for every occasion.

To taunt: "Go ahead, make my day." (*Dirty Harry*)

To express outrage: "I'm mad as hell, and I'm not going to take it anymore." (*Network*)

To show unease: "I have a feeling we're not in Kansas anymore." (*The Wizard of Oz*)

For all the crazy attitudes we have: "I love the smell of napalm in the morning." (*Apocalypse Now*)

To comment on relationships: "In every way but socially, you're my role model." (*Broadcast News*)

To express our philosophy of life: "Life is like a box of chocolates." (*Forrest Gump*)

To express our greatest desires: "I'll have what she's having." (*When Harry Met Sally*)

To justify our behavior: "I'm not bad, I'm just drawn that way." (*Who Killed Roger Rabbit*)

MAKE IT STRONG

The art and craft of great dialogue is making the words sing, echo, resonate, surprise, excite, and give insight to the human experience. The love of dialogue is the love of the power and music of words—their meanings and rhythms. It's finding the exact word, hitting the right note. In great dialogue, words and cinematic images are paired to give us a great depth of information about story, character, and theme.

Dialogue is not just chat. It's not just discussion. It's not just hanging out and shooting the breeze. It's also not about narrating a story or *talking about* things. Nor is it an opportunity for writers to share their philosophies of life. It should give only information that is relevant and *essential* to a story or the revelation of a character. Dialogue expresses a theme, reveals a character, implies a transformation, and helps clarify a character's transformation.

Good writers develop an ear for dialogue in the same way that musicians develop an ear for music. They listen. Like a philosopher searching for the perfect phrase to express an idea, the great writer searches for language's shadings and nuances. Writers intuit character's ulterior motives and subtext in much the same way psychologists listen for hidden meanings beneath their clients' words.

Unless you're an unusually gifted writer, great dialogue doesn't come easily. Writers must constantly work at finding and hearing the right word. They listen to how different people speak and listen to the patterns and rhythms and dialects and cultural nuances of speech. They listen to the languid rhythms of the cowboy in the West. They listen to the slow rhythms of the gracious Southerner. They listen to the clipped sounds of the Easterner. They hear all this as they would hear music.

They listen to their aunts, uncles, mothers, fathers, siblings, and friends. They listen to persuasive teachers and fire-and-brimstone preachers and the soft, quiet coos of the mother with her child.

Many writers tape-record some of the dialogue they hear. Many good writers read their dialogue aloud, seeking the right music for each character and the right rhythm for each scene. Some have read-throughs with actors so that they can hear what it sounds like when spoken by others. Dialogue, as Shakespeare said, should fall "trippingly on the tongue." It should be easily spoken. Like phrases in a song, it needs room for a breath. Words need to flow easily, one into the next, so the actor doesn't trip up on an alliteration or pronunciation or word combinations.

In college, I was in the chorus of the ancient Greek play *Hecuba* by Euripides. I had only one line of dialogue. I practiced and practiced but found no way to say it well. The line was "Surely, no man could be so calloused or so hard of heart that he could hear this woman's heart-broken cry and not be touched." After a number of rehearsals, the line was taken away from me and assigned to another chorus member, who had no more luck with it than I did. I wondered if anyone could deliver this line well. I could find no place to take a breath and still create an easy flow with the line. I knew my acting limits (I had gotten a "C" in acting), but I also knew that, sometimes, when dialogue is extraordinarily well-written, even the worst of actors become passable.

It has been said that Tennessee Williams wrote such brilliant dialogue that you could read it like you were reading a telephone book and it would still sound good. That was my experience: One of the few acting-class scenes I did that got compliments was playing a desperate and drunken lesbian in Williams' *Something Unspoken*. I knew that if I, a naïve young woman from northern Wisconsin, could pull that one off, the dialogue must be brilliant.

In my work as a script consultant, I come across a great deal of dialogue that has no sense of rhythm. It's wooden. It *does not* use contractions, and *is not* easily spoken. I come across dialogue that is bland, banal, trite, and too straightforward. It has no subtext. It doesn't sing. As a result, audiences don't believe the characters and don't believe the story.

DIALOGUE AS RHYTHM

Dialogue is rhythm. It's a rat-a-tat-tat, a bouncing tennis ball moving back and forth—bonk, bonk, bonk, and right back to you.

Dialogue has pace and rhythm. We talk fast, in a flow of words, or slowly, searching for each thought. Our words tell others whether we're loquacious or taciturn. The rhythm of our words tell others where we're from—north or south, east or west, one level of society or another. The energy behind our words tell others whether we're desparate or calm. Dialogue can set the style and period of an entire film through its rhythm and pace.

Listen to the rhythmic movement back and forth from *Witness*. "Drop the gun. Drop it. Drop the gun. Put the gun down, gun down, gun down."

Listen to dialogue from *Moonstruck*, where rhythm is established with short sentences, repetitive words, and alliteration.

>   RONNY
> They say bread is life. So I bake
> bread, bread, bread. And the years
> go by! By! By! And I sweat and
> shovel this stinkin' dough in and
> outta this hot hole in the wall and
> I should be so happy, huh, sweet-
> heart? You want me to come to the
> wedding of my brother Johnny?!!
> Where is my wedding? Chrissy! Over
> by the wall! Gimme the big knife
> ... I'm gonna cut my throat!"

In *Born on the Fourth of July*, the dialogue again relies on short and repetitive statements, capturing the desperate rhythms of confrontational and angry men.

>   CHARLIE
> They made me kill babies, man,
> little gook babies. You ever have
> to kill a baby?
>
>
>   RON
> Yeah. Okay. Come on, let's go ...
> let's get a ride ... let's get back
> to the villa.

```
                 CHARLIE
     Fuck you ... whaddaya mean okay ...
     whatdya mean okay — you ever kill a
     baby? You ever kill a little gook
     baby? Did you! Did you!


                 RON
     What?


                 CHARLIE
     Did you ever have to kill a baby?


                 RON
     No. No. I never killed a baby.


                 CHARLIE
     Yeah, I didn't think so. I didn't
     think so.
```

THE DIMENSIONS OF DIALOGUE

Just as musicians work with pitch, rhythm, pacing, and timbre to create pleasing musical patterns, writers have their own set of tools to create dialogue.

Just as a character has an external, an internal, and sometimes an invisible goal, good dialogue expresses all these levels of the character.

Dialogue's external dimension

Words and their conscious meanings form dialogue's external dimension. These words show the intent to the character. They tell us what we need to know and when we need to know it. They keep us focused on what is happening and why.

External dialogue moves a story forward with decisions, commands, and intentions. It's job is to clarify, for the audience, what's going on. It expresses the Who, What, When, Where, How, and sometimes the Why of a character. It's the information that we need in order to understand a story on its most basic levels—what's happening, who's doing what, why they're doing it, where they come from, where they're going, what they hope to gain, and what's the character's overall intention.

The beginning dialogue of *The Silence of the Lambs* delivers both story and character information. It answers many whos, whats, and whys.

WHO:

> CRAWFORD
> Starling, Clarice. Good morning.

WHAT:

> CRAWFORD
> A job's come up and I thought about
> you. Not really a job, more of — an
> interesting errand ... We're trying
> to interview all of the serial
> killers now in custody, for a
> psycho-behavioral profile.

WHY Clarice?

> CRAWFORD
> I remember you from my seminar at
> the University of Virginia ... I
> gave you an A.

> CLARICE
> A-minus.

> CRAWFORD
> You're qualified and available. And
> frankly, I can't spare a real agent
> right now.

WHO does he want her to meet?

> CLARICE
> Who's the subject?

                    CRAWFORD
          The psychiatrist - Dr. Hannibal
          Lecter.

                     CLARICE
          Hannibal, the cannibal.

WHAT does he want her to do and HOW does he want
her to do it?

                    CRAWFORD
          I don't expect him to talk to you,
          but I have to be able to say we
          tried ... if he won't cooperate,
          then just straight reporting. How's
          he look, how's the cell look,
          what's he writing?

And then Emotional Information is added for suspense and
tension.

WHY does she need to be careful?

                    CRAWFORD
          Be very careful with Hannibal Lecter
          ... You tell him nothing personal,
          Starling. Believe me, you don't want
          Hannibal Lecter inside your head ...
          just do your job but never forget
          what he is ... a monster.

And then we get another little tidbit of character information about Clarice and Hannibal when Chilton tells her —

                    CHILTON
          And, oh, are you ever his taste, so
          to speak!

Dialogue that expresses intention

In almost every film, some of the dialogue expresses a
character's intention. In most scripts, this appears within the
setup or, at the latest, at the end of Act One.

In *Bull Durham*, Annie tells Crash and Ebby her plan. And Crash tells her and the audience about himself.

                    ANNIE
     These are the ground rules (beat).
     I hook up with one guy a season — I
     mean it takes me a couple of weeks
     to pick the guy — kinda my own
     spring training ... (beat) And,
     well, you two are the most promis-
     ing prospects of the season so far.
                    (beat)
     So ... I thought we should get to
     know each other.

                    CRASH
     Why do you get to choose? Why don't
     I get to choose? Why doesn't he get
     to choose?

                    ANNIE
     Actually, none of us on this planet
     ever really choose each other. It's
     all Quantum Physics and molecular
     attraction. There are laws we don't
     understand that bring us together
     and break us apart ...

                    EBBY
     Is somebody gonna go to bed with
     somebody or what?

                    ANNIE:
     You're a regular nuclear meltdown,
     honey — cool off a little.

     (Crash rises to leave)

                    ANNIE
     Where are you going? I barely got
     started.

                    CRASH
        After twelve years in the minor
        league, I don't try out. Besides, I
        don't believe half the garbage com-
        ing out of your mouth.

                    ANNIE
        Only half? What do you believe in?

Annie's question slightly taunting. He stops and speaks with
both aloofness and passion.

                    CRASH
        I believe in the soul, the cock,
        the pussy, the small of a woman's
        back, the hanging curve ball, high
        fiber, good scotch, long foreplay,
        show tunes, and that the novels of
        Thomas Pynchon are self-indulgent,
        overrated crap.

                    (beat)

        I believe that Lee Harvey Oswald
        acted alone. I believe that there
        oughtta be a constitutional amend-
        ment outlawing astro-turf and the
        designated hitter. I believe in
        the "sweet spot," voting every
        election, soft-core pornography,
        chocolate chip cookies, opening
        your presents on Christmas morning
        rather than Christmas Eve, and I
        believe in long, slow, deep, soft,
        wet kisses that last for three
        days.

                    ANNIE
                  (breathless)

        Oh, my ...

Clarifying motivation

In most scripts, characters clarify their motivations for doing
what they do. In *Dangerous Liaisons*, Marquise de Merteuil
clarifies the reason for her cruel and manipulative scheme.
She explains her desires to Valmont, hoping that he will enjoy her scheme as much as she does.

> MARQUISE DE MERTEUIL
> Do you know why I summoned you here
> this morning? ... I need you to
> carry out a heroic enterprise ...

She explains her desire: She wants "revenge" against Bastide.
She explains her motivation for choosing Bastide: He's her
former lover who left her. And she explains why she has con-
cocted her scheme: Bastide wants to marry the virgin Cécile
de Volanges, because "his priority, you see, is a guaranteed
virtue." Marquise de Merteuil intends to make sure that the
virtue Bastide expects will be compromised by Valmont's
sleeping with Cécile.

But Valmont isn't sure he wants to be part of de Merteuil's
gameplan.

> VALMONT
> No, I can't ... it's too easy ... I
> have my reputation to think of.

Valmont has his own gameplan. He wants to seduce the very
virtuous Madame de Tourvel. He explains why he chooses
de Tourvel above Cécile:

> VALMONT
> To seduce a woman famous for strict
> morals, religious fervour, and the
> happiness of her marriage. What
> could possibly be more prestigious?
> I want the excitement of watching
> her betray everything that's most
> important to her. Surely you under-
> stand that. I thought betrayal was
> your favourite word.

```
          MARQUISE DE MERTEUIL
     No, cruelty. I always think that
     has a nobler ring to it.
```

Valmont and de Merteuil's evil, driving intentions are the engines for the entire story, eventually destroying both characters and those around them. The writer has masterfully layered the dialogue to answer all the motivational questions, and to direct the journey of the story.

Setting up the context

Dialogue needs to set up the world inhabited by a film's characters—the context in which they live. Dialogue in combination with images set up the characters' occupations, period, locations, and cultures.

Some context is revealed through the character's vocabulary. By our choice of words, we all convey who we are, telling others about our educational background, economic level, occupation, country, region, and much more. Are our words big or small? What kind of grammar do we use?

A doctor's occupation might be expressed by the use of medical language. A cop might use law-enforcement slang. Occupations might be expressed through the languages of archaeology, aviation, editing, writing, ranching, or farming.

The film *Notting Hill* has a charming scene that makes fun of the sometimes obscure contextual dialogue we find in certain films. William, the bookseller, is helping actress Anna with her lines for her next film. He asks her, "Basic plot?"

```
                    ANNA
     I'm a difficult but brilliant
     junior officer who in about twenty
     minutes will save the world from
     nuclear disaster ...


                  WILLIAM
     Message from command. Would you
     like them to send in the HKs?
```

> ANNA
> No, turn over four TRs and tell
> them we need radar feedback before
> the KFTs return at nineteen hundred
> — then inform the Pentagon that
> we'll be needing black star cover
> from ten hundred through 12.15.

If dialogue is so weighted down with vocabulary that it's not understandable to the ordinary person, some translation is needed in order for the audience to understand it. Often this translation is given visually. We see the scalpel when the doctor asks for it. We see a legal brief or we see a scene of an attorney taking a deposition or we see the strange-sounding chemical as it's carefully handled or transported. If Anna's new film were actually produced, we'd undoubtedly see some KFTs and we'd notice when the black star cover comes into play between 10:00 and 12:15.

Conveying the culture through dialogue

Good dialogue conveys a sense of a character's culture and environment. In *Moonstruck, My Left Foot, The Full Monty, Billy Elliot,* and *The Color Purple*, dialogue gives us the flavor of the culture and the geographical location.

Often, dialogue includes slang that is part of a culture or occupation. Many writers read slang books when working on specific subject matter. For a nautical film, they probably need to know words such as "galley" and "brig" and "head" and "bilge." If writing a cowboy film, a writer may need to know about the "latigo" and "billet" and "cantle." For films about horses, a writer would need to know the difference between a "lope" and a "hand gallop," and what it means if the horse is on the wrong "lead" or the rider is on the wrong "diagonal." For a theatre film, a writer would need to know what's "the green room" and what it means to move "stage right" or "stage left."

Dialogue shows cultural differences. The taciturn American cowboy flavor of *Unforgiven*:

MUNNY
(to his son, Bill)
Before I met your ma, God rest her
soul, it used to be I was kinda ...
wicked ... drinkin' spirits an'
gettin' into scrapes an' all. Only
she made me see the error of my ways
an' ... I ain't like I was no more.

The Irish flavor of *My Left Foot*:

MR. BROWN
Give me a pint and a chaser there,
Brian.

FRIEND
Congratulations.

MR. BROWN
On what?

FRIEND
The new boy, Christy.

MR. BROWN
Are you trying to make a jackass
out of me or what? The child's an
imbecile. A moron. A vegetable. I
says to the doctor, 'Is there any
hope for him?' and the doctor says,
'Well, Mr. Brown, there is some
movement in his left foot.' His
left foot! He'll never be able to
pick up a trowel or mend a gable
wall. He's shagged good and proper
... I'll tell you one thing,
though, that's the end of the road
for me in the breeding stakes.

FRIEND
How will you manage that?

>   MR. BROWN
>   Abstinence.

The Southern flavor of *The Color Purple:*

>   SHUG
>   You know, Celie, God love every-
>   thing you love, and a mess of stuff
>   you don't ... I think it pisses God
>   off if you just walk by the color
>   purple in a field and don't notice
>   it.

>   CELIE
>   You mean it want to be loved, like
>   the Bible said.

>   SHUG
>   Yes, Celie, everything wants to be
>   loved. Us sing and dance, make
>   faces, give flower bouquets ...
>   Just trying to be loved ...

The Full Monty's sounds of the industrial north of England:

>   ALAN
>   Oi, Patricia the Stripper, where
>   you bloody been?

>   GAZ
>   What's it to you?

>   ALAN
>   Well, what's goin' on? I've had to
>   buy in twenty barrels and I've
>   heard not a peep from you ...
>   You're bloody famous.

The Catholic culture of *Moonstruck:*

>   LORETTA
>   Bless me, Father, for I have sinned
>   ...

```
                    PRIEST
        What sins have you to confess?


                    LORETTA
        Twice I took the name of God in
        vain, once I slept with the brother
        of my fiancé, and once I bounced a
        check at the liquor store ...


                    PRIEST
        What was that second thing you
        said, Loretta?
```

Sometimes, dialogue gives us a sense of a character's educational background, which may be a surprise.

In *Taxi Driver*, there's a scene where Wizard tells Travis that he's no Bertram Russell. We don't expect Wizard to know philosophers. In *Pulp Fiction*, we don't expect the killer Jules to be religious and to quote Ezekiel, and to try to be "a better shepherd." In *Bull Durham*, we don't expect Annie to mention quantum physics.

From dialogue's external dimension, we get the facts and a liberal dose of character detailing, which includes rhythm and vocabulary. But a character also needs depth, which comes from a writer's knowledge of a character's internal and invisible dimensions.

Dialogue's internal dimension

Dialogue's internal dimension expresses a character's psychology. This dialogue is often designed to hide as much as to reveal the elements that make a character tick. These include the secrets that a character doesn't want anyone to know and the fears that a character tries to hide. A character knows his or her own wants and fears, but isn't telling anyone. A character tries to hide who s/he really is, but dialogue gives us glimpses into a character's true identity. It expresses a character's needs and motivations and yearnings and desires.

The "Why" that I discussed in Chapter 8 still motivates the character, but to it we add an *inner motivation*, a personal, internal desire that drives the character.

We can look in several directions to find a character's inner motivation. We can look for life's transition points. Perhaps a character is at a transition point in her life—moving from conformity to creativity or from materialism to a spiritual perspective or from isolation to intimacy or from failure to success. The character is moving because life is pushing for change. The story has set the change in motion.

We can take any one of the transitions discussed in Chapter 9 and build an arc from the negative to the positive. A film might show a child moving from low self-esteem to self-confidence or an adult from materialism to spirituality or from isolation to intimacy. If a character's desire is conscious, the character will often express that desire, revealing the psychology that drives him or her, and then take action to fulfill that desire.

In *American Beauty*, Lester expresses his desire to change:

```
              LESTER (V.O.)
    Both my wife and daughter think I'm
    this gigantic loser and ... they're
    right ... I have lost something.
    I'm not exactly sure what it is,
    but I know I didn't always feel
    this ... sedated. But you know
    what? It's never too late to get it
    back.
```

These lines in Act One set up the story track, the thematic line, and begin the character's transformational arc. They express Lester's understanding of where he is now in his life and express his intention to change. By the beginning of Act Two, Lester admits that he's changing.

Dialogue expresses subtext

Without subtext, everyone says exactly what they mean and characters have no layers. They have no mystery. They have no psychological depth. We get no feeling for the complexities of a character. Without subtext, dialogue is on-the-nose. It's obvious. Often it's a cliché. And without subtext, dialogue can become preachy and characters can become cardboard mouthpieces for a writer. Mastering subtext is one of the most important skills for the screenwriter. Without subtext, characters will never come to life and actors will have few dimensions to play.

Sometimes a character's psychological drive is expressed through subtext. We could define subtext as what a character really means, even though s/he might actually say something quite different. Subtext might be called the meaning under or behind the text or the meaning between the lines. Sometimes characters know the subtext they're communicating, although they hide it from others.

Sometimes, a character *intends* to convey a particular meaning to another character, even though his or her words might state quite the opposite.

"What's wrong, honey?" she says to her silent, brooding spouse.

"Nothing."

Clearly something is wrong, but he's not telling her. He might not be telling her because he doesn't want to talk about it or beecause he may not know exactly what's wrong, although he probably knows something is wrong.

If you asked him, he might tell you that he's "just a little tired," although we—and he—know it's more than that. The subtext is the rest. What's really wrong? A whole series of things, but he's only conscious of some of them. Subtext tells us the truth. When it's conscious, the character knows the truth, but isn't saying it.

In *The Accidental Tourist*, Muriel invites Macon over for dinner. He says, "Oh. Well, I could come. If it's only for dinner." And she responds, "What else would it be for?" We know, and she knows, that she's interested in him. But she's not saying it. Her ulterior motive lies under the surface of her response.

Sometimes subtext is used for irony: "I only want to hurt him a little" says the hitman, as he lovingly fingers his AK-47. Clearly, the desire to hurt is there. But we know it's not to hurt him a little, the desire is to hurt him a lot.

The character's hidden subtext

Usually subtext is invisible to the main character, and often to all of the story's characters. The difference between internal subtext and invisible subtext has to do with whether the character is conscious of the truth. If the character is conscious of the truth, it's an internal subtext. If the character is unconscious of the truth, it's an invisible subtext. If someone said to you, "I love you," you might answer, "And I love you." If you mean it, it's a conscious truth. However, you might not mean it but say it anyway, avoiding eye contact with the person, thereby revealing the line's subtext—which is, "I don't love you but am afraid to say so." You know the truth but feel you can't convey it to the other person. Or you might not realize that you really don't mean it. In many films, characters think that they're a loving husband or wife as they abuse their spouse or disrespect them or insult them. The truth about their relationship is invisible to them, but it's boiling underneath the surface. It stays hidden until another character or an event or some stress forces the subtext to be revealed. Great subtext, however, is not invisible to the audience. The audience knows what's going on, even when no one in a film does.

When the truth is unconscious to a character, the character may be in denial or doesn't understand or isn't aware of the invisible, unconscious forces that bubble beneath the surface.

Sometimes the hidden subtext slips out against a character's wishes. Sometimes dialogue uses an object or a prop to convey the hidden subtext. In *Ordinary People*, as the grandparents try to take a Christmas photograph, there's a great deal of discussion and confrontation about who will be in the picture, whether they'll smile, who will take the picture. It's clear that the frustration is not about the photography, but about the dysfunction within the family. Finally Calvin, the father, shouts, "Give her the goddamn camera!" By the time the photo is finally taken, Conrad has turned away from his parents, his body language clearly visualizing the problem.

From a writer's mind to the characters words

Sometimes writers have specific ideas, insights, and wisdom they want to express through their characters. These may be words of wisdom that they want to convey to the audience, hoping they'll have a transforming influence on the audience. This kind of dialogue, if not done adeptly, can feel as if it's preaching to us. If done well, it can encourage a character, and lead to that character's transformation. It can be words that help a character find inner balance and insight. As the character achieves understanding, we in the audience also get the message.

In *On Golden Pond,* Ethel is a voice of wisdom who tries to help her grandson understand the insensitive behavior of his grandfather.

```
                    ETHEL
         Sometimes you have to look hard at
         a person and remember that he is
         doing the best he can. He is just
         trying to find his way. That's all.
         Just like you.
```

Sometimes dialogue is used by one character to encourage another. This kind of dialogue can be a testament to the care that one person can have for another.

Katherine, the piano teacher in *Shine*, encourages David and lets him know that she understands his talents.

>   KATHERINE
> Each time you play "Sospiro" it
> expresses so completely ... The
> inexpressible.

>   DAVID
> Is that good?

>   KATHERINE
> It's divine.

Sometimes one character's encouragement leads another character to new behavior. In *Babe*, the sheep explain to Babe that wolf-like violent behavior isn't necessary, even though Fly, the dog, has her own opinion of how to herd sheep.

>   FLY
> Make them feel inferior ... Abuse
> them! Insult them!

>   BABE
> They'll laugh at me.

>   FLY
> Then bite them! ... Be ruthless!
> Whatever it takes! Bend them to
> your will!

>   BABE
> Move along there, you you b-b-
> bloody b-buggers!

> The sheep can't contain themselves. They
> erupt in hysterical laughter. Babe glares
> with as much venom as he can muster, runs
> at the nearest sheep, and bites her on the
> leg. She squeals.

```
          MAA'S VOICE
          (indignant)

   Babe! Stop this nonsense ... What's
   got into you?


             BABE
   I'm sorry, Maa. I wanted to be a
   sheep dog.


             MAA
   No need for all this wolf nonsense,
   Babe. All a nice little chap like
   you need do is ask.


With Babe walking beside them, the flock,
in ORDERLY FORMATION, proceeds calmly to-
ward the open gate.


             BABE
          (to sheep)

   Thanks very much. Very kind of you.


        VARIOUS SHEEP
      (chorus of comments)

   A pleasure! Thank you, young 'un.
   What a nice little chap!
```

Great writers write and rewrite their dialogue, honing it, saying it out loud, shaping the rhythms, sometimes using alliteration and rhymes. Once they know who a character is and how s/he talks, they've taken an important step toward creating an imaginative cinematic world for the character to inhabit.

11

Creating a Style

M ost films strive for realism. Kitchens look like our own kitchens, except maybe a little bit bigger. Offices look like our own. Cars might be a little fancier than most of ours, but they're recognizable. Champagne and wine look like what we drink, although film characters often drink the more expensive brand.

A writer decides just how realistic to make a story. Do we see people eating in their kitchens, scraping food, loading dishwashers, and putting dishes away? Do we see the bullet enter and the wound spurt out blood? Do we hear the ping of the bullet, as in *Boyz N the Hood*? Do we hear the sounds of battle or do they get muted, as in *Born on the Fourth of July*. Do we see the lovers in ordinary surroundings or in glamorized silhouette, as in *Bugsy*?

Some films are deliberately not realistic. Robert Altman, the Coen brothers, David Lynch, Baz Luhrmann in *Moulin Rouge!*, Roberto Benigni in *Life Is Beautiful* all create styles that define them as quirky or visionary artists who push us into new realities. How do they do it?

THE POINT OF VIEW

Style is established through a filmmaker's point of view. An audience is shown a world from a *specific perspective*: idealistic, romantic, child-like, optimistic, pessimistic, cynical, or despairing. A writer establishes this point of view by creating a specific lens through which we see the world of the story. The director further interprets the writer's point of view through visual expressions of character and plot.

A film's world might be seen through rose-colored glasses or gray-colored glasses or through a distorted lens. Everything might be spectacular, as in *Moulin Rouge!* Or a writer might create the dark and edgy and corrupt world, as in *L.A. Confidential.* Perhaps a writer presents a hopeful and good-humored world, where characters are always optimistic, even in the face of adversity. We see this positive world in such films as *Chocolate* and *Babe.* Style is not so much about events themselves but about how a writer interprets events.

This lesson about interpretation was brought home to me rather powerfully in the late 1990s when my mother informed me that we had been poor when I was young. This came as a complete surprise to me, since I thought we had been middle-class, perhaps even upper-middle-class. I couldn't think of anything that proved our poverty. In our living room, we had a Steinway Concert Grand piano, which seemed to be proof of our wealth. When I asked my mother to explain this, she told me that the Steinway was given to her, to be paid off whenever she could, because a wealthy man had admired her piano playing and wanted her to have the piano after his wife died. Mother explained to me that she had been determined not to bring us up with the poverty complex that she had had. So she simply *interpreted* events for us through a positive point of view that told us that everything was all right and the world was a good place to be. When we had hot dogs for Thanksgiving one year, she didn't tell us that we didn't have any money, but told us that we were going to have something special and different for dinner that year. We thought that was grand! When other little girls had new dresses at Christmas, Mother explained that since some children didn't have new dresses, we didn't want to make them feel bad. She suggested we wear our pretty dresses from last year. Ah, yes, that seemed to make perfect sense. From my mother's revelations, I realized how much our lives are about interpretation.

Interpretation is style. It's the way the writer and the director, working together, interpret the world for us.

CREATING STYLE THROUGH CHARACTER

Some writers focus their lenses on the outskirts of life, on the strange distortions that are a part of humanity. Robert Altman's character-driven films offer a unique peek into the quirkiness of life. Altman's world *looks* similar to ours—kitchens, restaurants, living rooms are all recognizable—but what his characters do within them establishes his trademark style. In Altman's films, most, if not all, of his characters are quirky and have a similar slant on life.

In Altman's *Short Cuts,* a telephone sex operator effortlessly changes her child's diapers while keeping her client erotically charged. In his *Dr. T and the Women,* Richard Gere is able to carry on the most intimate aspects of a gynecological exam while socializing with his patient—who also happens to be his buddy's wife. It's these strange juxtapositions that define Altman's style, which depends on showing the onscreen world as normal, while the audience knows it's not.

Sometimes a writer chooses only one character to set a whole film's style. In *Life Is Beautiful,* we see the world through the child-like, charming, and delightful point of view of Guido, who echoes his son's point of view. He encourages his son to maintain this point of view in spite of circumstances. Although his immediate world is filled with tragedy, by seeing with the wondrous eyes of a child, Guido is able to interpret events so his child sees the world as fun and charming, rather than filled with horror and evil.

Every event in the film is interpreted through eyes of wonder. When the Nazis put up a sign that says, "No Jews allowed," Guido clarifies what it really means from a child's perspective. When Guido wants his son to hide, he makes it into a child-like game. Even at the concentration camp, Guido manages to bring laughter, music, and fun into this bleak world.

When creating style through character, at least one character has to set the tone, and that tone must remain constant from start to finish. Every scene in *Life Is Beautiful* had to keep its light touch, no matter how tragic the circumstances. When Guido and Dora run away, they do so on a green horse. Even though the horse has anti-Jewish slogans written on its side, the sense of magic of the green horse keeps Guido's tone of wonder. Even when Guido goes to his death, he does it with a high-step march and a salute to his son. Imagine if a writer decided to show Guido being executed. The tone would have changed. Imagine if Guido allowed the Nazis to force him into despair. This would have completely changed the style of a film, which worked so well because it never lost its light-hearted charm.

CREATING STYLE THROUGH STORY AND CHARACTER

Some writers and directors, such as the Coen brothers, create their style through a combination of character and story. In *Raising Arizona*, a hellish-looking motorcyclist almost runs over a little baby—but not quite. Escaped convicts comically claw their way out of their escape tunnel, ending up in what seems to be the middle of nowhere. The main character, an incorrigible repeat criminal, marries his correctional officer.

In *Fargo*, everything is pushed a notch. Most of the characters speak with a Midwestern Scandinavian accent. These homespun characters respond to almost any comment with "you betcha" and "thanks a bunch." Girls describe the thugs as "kinda funny looking," which is probably just about as helpful a description as some real cops get, but here it's used for humor and irony.

Fargo's point of view depends on the story's outrageousness and the naivete that comes from characters who don't see the full picture. In *Fargo*, every character sees the world with a certain degree of innocence. This is not a child-like innocence, but an innocence that comes from a limited world view. Jerry, a hapless car dealer who hires kidnappers, sees the world through such a self-centered Jerry-lens that he is unable to foresee the consequences of his actions. He is trapped by his limited thinking, and some of the film's black comedy comes from his inadequate point of view. Gaear and Carl's naivete renders them blind to all the potential problems of their crime and the obvious mistake of working with Jerry. They, like Jerry, are incompetent at their jobs. And, like Jerry, they simply don't know it.

Marge, a very warm-hearted, pregnant cop, sees the world through an always-positive outlook, so she also doesn't see the big picture. She loves her cozy world with her husband and the baby to come. She can't foresee Mikey's deception and doesn't understand why someone would put his accomplice in the woodchipper on such a beautiful day.

In *Fargo,* the events that form its storyline occur as a result of a pervasively innocent point of view. If Jerry could have foreseen the consequences, he would have made different decisions, thereby forming a different storyline. If Carl and Gaear had a less limited point of view of the world, they would never have agreed to work with Jerry, thereby changing the storyline.

CREATING STYLE THROUGH IMAGE

Some films, such as *Moulin Rouge!,* are drenched with color and energy and music and dance and glitter and sparkle and pizzazz. In the world of *Moulin Rouge!,* nothing appears normal. The writer, the director, and the actors push everything over the top. It is hyper-dramatic, bordering on the surreal. Actors overreact. No move is casual. When love is in the air, fireworks magically go off behind the lovers. A huge heart in the set design establishes the love theme. Wild costumes and makeup offer a hyper-reality. Even Satine's illness—consumption—is played with the maximum amount of romance and the energy of an Olympic skater. For those of us who've read about Elizabeth Barrett Browning's consumption, during which she languished in her bed in London, we had no idea that someone could dance, sing, shimmy, purr, growl, make wild love, and still be consumptive. Even Satine's coughed-up blood is a pretty red color, in a perfect aesthetic pattern, against her white linen handkerchief.

Moulin Rouge! shows us a multi-genre through the combination of the theatrical lenses of musical comedy, nineteenth-century opera, and the 1930s and 1940s Hollywood musical. Like a stage musical, characters sing when they're happy, sad, in love, or in great jeopardy, and they even manage to get out a last whisper of song when they're just about dead.

The music in *Moulin Rouge!* does not correspond to its historical setting, the turn of the century. It's modern music, including "Like a Virgin," "Up Where We Belong," "Diamonds are a Girl's Best Friend," "Come What May," and songs from *The Sound of Music*. This music makes it clear that the film is not based in reality. We're expected to suspend disbelief and not notice that these songs were written fifty to a hundred years later than the period of a film.

Some theatrical musicals have unsuccessfully been turned into films: for example, *Man of La Mancha*, *Chorus Line*, *Godspell*, *Jesus Christ Superstar*, and *Evita*. These films didn't succeed because they worked *against* the intrinsically theatrical style of the musical, becoming too realistic and, therefore, seemingly more banal. The hyper-real fire and energy of these theatrical musicals was gone. With *Moulin Rouge!*, director Luhrmann immediately lets us know all is make-believe. He shows us the overture played by an orchestra in front of the stage curtain, conducted by an enthusiastic conductor. Then the camera leads us into the magical world of the Moulin Rouge. Luhrmann's style consistently tells us that this is the world of theater. From distorted faces to strange makeup, we're never allowed to believe that anything here is really real.

Moulin Rouge!'s style works on two levels. It distances us with its period anachronisms of song, story, and its theatrical use of color and space, letting us know that this is theater-turned-into-film. Yet it pulls us into its story with its intense emotions and complex relationships. It is emotionally serious and theatrically playful. It's been called "hip, sexy, and outrageous," and that it is. And in my view, Luhrmann made it work, and it works beautifully. Every camera shot, every turn of the head, every closeup and long-shot, every intersection of music, dance, fireworks, change of lighting, change of color—every detail—works together to create an exciting film tapestry of sound and image.

A similar style was used in the film *Chicago*. Its style is darker than *Moulin Rouge!* and featured blues and grays and black shadows, rather than the bright colors of *Moulin Rouge!*. It's film noir set to music. Yet, like *Moulin Rouge!*, it is also theatrical and playful. When the lawyer, Billy Flynn, has to save his client, he literally tap dances around the little problem that she is guilty of murdering her lover. Characters sing and dance their passions, their betrayals, their seductions, with sparkles and spangles and plenty of glitter.

I didn't believe that film could create a truly theatrical feeling. I'm pleased that I was proven wrong two years in a row. *Moulin Rouge!* and *Chicago* expanded film's stylistic possibilities and created a new film "language" that could, potentially, prove a model for successful versions of *Phantom of the Opera* or the musical of *Les Misérables* or any number of other theatrical pieces that have never been brought to the screen.

CREATING STYLE THROUGH GENRES

Action-adventures, thrillers, and romances usually look much like the world we know around us. However, such genres as film noir and magic realism express a decidedly non-realistic style. They are worlds of sharp constrasts: the dark and the light, the edgy and the hopeful, spirituality and sensuality, destiny and fate.

Much of what I've learned about film noir and magic realism I've learned from my friend and colleague Sharon Y. Cobb, a professional screenwriter who has written both neo-noir and magic-realism scripts, as well as written articles and given lectures about these two styles. Sharon defines film noir:

> Film noir reflects our nightmares. It's edgy and dark.
> We often see images of wet streets at night. Flashing
> neon in the window of a seedy bar. Smoke-filled
> rooms. They reflect the dramatic contrasts between
> light and shadow, the stark symbols of isolation.
>
> The themes are about betrayal, alienation, despera-
> tion. The stories symbolize our darkest ruminations,
> our worst fears. Black is not black, and white is not
> white. Noir takes place in the morally ambiguous
> world of crime where the main character often is the
> criminal, or the corrupt cop.

Modern film noir is sometimes called neo-noir, a genre that includes such films as *Chinatown, Body Heat, Jagged Edge, Blue Velvet, The Grifters, Basic Instinct, Reservoir Dogs, Pulp Fiction, The Usual Suspects, Fargo, Seven, L.A. Confidential,* and *Memento,* among others.

A highly stylized genre, such as film noir, is determined by its subject matter and its approach to that subject. Compare the edginess of *The Maltese Falcon* or *Double Indemnity* with the more realistic cop films *The Fugitive* or *Witness.* The themes of the latter films are about integrity and fighting corruption—classic good-versus-evil, with certain characters clearly being the good guys. However, in the world of film noir where things are not always as they seem, it's not unusual for the main character to be almost as bad as the bad guys. According to Sharon:

This is the world of the double-cross. In *Body Heat*, Matty convinces Racine to kill her husband, then double-crosses him. In *L.A. Confidential*, Bud is willing to assault whomever Dudley asks him to. And Exley, at the end, is willing to take part in the morally ambiguous world, and find a way to fit his rules into that world. Jerry Lundegaard, William Macy's character in *Fargo*, betrays his father-in-law and his wife by staging the wife's kidnapping, hoping to collect ransom from the father-in-law, until things go very wrong.

Many of these films are sexy and erotic, with a femme-fatale character who is the main character's only source of hope. She represents a way out of his current nightmarish life. She is usually wealthy, beautiful, intelligent, and elusive. But the femme fatale always has her own agenda, and after using the protagonist for her own gains, she will deceive him. An example is Kim Basinger's character in *L.A. Confidential* who is a victim of her own beauty and serves as a Veronica Lake look-alike callgirl. She lures Bud into a sexual relationship, but then betrays him by having a sexual encounter with Bud's fellow detective, who is photographed and blackmailed.

In *Basic Instinct*, Nick is attracted to Tramell and risks his life, knowing she's a murder suspect, to satisfy his obsession with her. Sex and violence collide in this symbiotic codependency between the anti-hero and the femme fatale.

Whereas film noir is dark and edgy, magic realism presents a world that is lighter. In this world, extraordinary events take place in an ordinary world, but these events are often perceived to be ordinary by the characters and narrator.

When Sharon teaches magic realism, she uses examples from several Academy Award-nominated films.

In magical realism, events and characters are pushed to be bigger than life and exaggerated. In *Like Water for Chocolate*, when Tita lights candles to meet her lover, there aren't three candles, or five, but fifty or a hundred. When Gertrudis escapes with the man she loves, she does it naked, coming out of the shower, and leaps on his horse to go off and become a revolutionary.

What seems impossible in the real world is not only possible in the magical realism world but accepted as common. In *Crouching Tiger, Hiden Dragon*, it is commonplace for warriors to fly through the air and balance on tree tops during their battles.

Natural elements and sensuality play a strong role in this genre. In *Chocolate*, Vianne, along with her daughter, are literally blown into the repressed little French town. Her chocolate confections awaken passions in the townsfolk they haven't felt for years.

Creating a style through genre demands a thorough knowledge of how the genre works, and then choosing theme, characters, storyline, and images to fit its particular world view.

CREATING STYLE BY MIXING GENRES

Some styles are created through a mixing of genres: comedy and horror, comedy and drama, sci-fi comedy, or sci-fi thriller. *Fargo* could be considered neo-noir, yet it contains a lot of humor. *Prizzi's Honor* is a black comedy. The remake of *King Kong* was meant to be a horror spoof played as camp, but it didn't work, partly because different actors were playing different styles.

Some writers mix genres by starting out with one, adding another, and then shifting back and forth between them. This method can cause a script to feel like the scenes are self-contained pieces merely tacked together. When mixing genres, in most cases, both genres need to be set up at the same time. Early in my career, I worked on a comic horror script (which didn't get made). I remember suggesting to the writer that he put comedy and horror in the first scene in order to establish the style immediately. Since it started with a beheading, I suggested that he find something funny to add, such as the head wearing a headband that reads "Peace and Love, Brother." I encouraged the writer to to try come up with a number of humorous details that might alert us immediately to the presence of humor mixed with horror.

In very rare cases, it's possible to switch genres part way through a film. *Terms of Endearment* begins as a comedy and gradually becomes more dramatic and even tragic. It successfully moves from comedy to drama, but I have not yet seen a film move successfuly from drama to comedy. I do believe that it could be done if subtle comedic touches were established immediately, and then there were subtle shifts into comedy as the film progressed.

In *Mighty Aphrodite*, Woody Allen combines the genres of the drama with the conventions of the Greek tragedy, using the device of a Greek chorus to set up the film's themes and to make its story seem more ironic, more miraculous, more wondrous, and more important than it really is. Masked chorus figures provide a running commentary that warns us of danger, the workings of fate, the threat of hubris, and the importance of getting tickets to the Knicks game. They sing. They dance. They play with mythic Greek figures, such as the blind Tiresias who says he *saw* Amanda. And at the end, the chorus sings "When You're Smiling" and goes into a dance, gleeful at the irony that the two major characters have each other's child but don't know it.

A writer chooses the style that best expresses his or her interpretation of life or interpretation of a character's journey. If done well, style adds to a film's entertainment value and lends visual spark, but, most importantly, it helps a film connect with the audience.

12

The Roar
of the Crowd

Your stories, your themes, your characters—why do you create them? If you've read this far, you've realized that I'm not talking about writing screenplays simply for self-expression or for therapy or just to have something to do. I'm talking about writing in order to communicate with an audience. You write screenplays because, ultimately, you want an audience to be touched and moved and to respond to what you've done. Perhaps, like many writers, you want to change the world, and you find writing for film and television one of the best and most powerful ways to do this.

Every idea discussed in the preceeding eleven chapters ultimately will affect an audience's responses to your film.

Why should you care that your catalyst is clear and your turning points well-placed and well-crafted? So the audience gets oriented to your story and stays focused throughout the film. Why should you care that your theme be explored? So the audience gets the idea you're trying to communicate and is enriched by your themes. Why does it matter that your characters are multi-dimensional and move beyond stereotypes? So the audience understands them and identifies with them. So that your characters have the power to move an audience—whether to laughter and chuckles and smiles and grins or to weeping, sniffling, and sobbing.

Above all, don't you want to touch, mesmerize, hold, transform, and entertain an audience? Don't you want to create magic and wonder, so the audience leaves the theater feeling good about the two hours spent in the presence of your characters as they journey through your story?

What do you think about the audience—for whom you work and play and write?

DUMBING DOWN TO THE AUDIENCE

Some writers believe that the audience is about a D+ student. This stance can lead them to write films in which the story and characters are dumbed down. Would you stay in a dangerous haunted house, night after night, in spite of a threat to your survival, even though you had enough money and enough friends to leave? Probably not. But Michelle Pfeiffer did in *What Lies Beneath*. Would any reasonably aware woman walk down a dark alley or street by herself in an area known for its high crime rate? No, but hundreds of women do almost nightly on television. Would a reasonably smart detective turn his back on a fallen murderer who still holds a gun in his hand? No, but hundreds of movie detectives have done it, from the classic films to the most contemporary—and they usually get shot in the process. Would beautiful Michelle Pfeiffer fall in love with a man who is thirty years older than her, who lacks wit, charm, sensitivity, and romance—and who turns into a wolf? Not in real life, but in *Wolf* she did.

In these examples, the writer not only denies our intelligence but our common sense too. Writers of these films must have thought that we wouldn't notice a character's stupidity. They didn't seem to understand that audience members distance themselves from the unbelievable and the incredible.

THE CONDESCENDING STANCE

Some writers figure that they're so much smarter than the audience that they write deliberately obtuse films to stroke their own egos. In their minds, they're superior to their audience. They think that their movies always work and that any perceived unclarities are the fault of critics' and audiences' diminished mental capacities, not the writers' art or craft.

Why can't anyone figure out *Mulholland Drive?* Is this a good thing, that it never adds up in spite of so many moments of brilliance? Some critics and audience members loved the fact that it seemed like a puzzle. We've been watching movie puzzles for years and are mesmerized by their complexity. But even the critics couldn't put this puzzle together in a coherent way. The pieces didn't fit to create a whole.

In many obtuse films, writers seem to throw everything into the mix, without carefully selecting only those elements that serve a film and clearly aid the communication of its themes. Sometimes this lack of selectivity comes from self-indulgence. Sometimes it comes from ego.

Just how clear does a writer need to be? Clear enough that an audience can understand the story from beginning to end. Just how smart should we expect the audience to be? At least as smart as the writer—maybe smarter. Does this mean a writer has to sacrifice artistry for clarity? No. A writer can be both subtle and clear. Both artistic and focused. Respect for the audience doesn't preclude artistry and mystery.

KNOWING YOUR INTENDED AUDIENCE

A writer needs to know his or her intended audience. Who is the target audience for a particular script? Teenaged boys? Women? Sports fans? Intellectuals? Hard-core gore and horror fans?

What issues will the intended audience be confronting at this time in their lives? What are their concerns, struggles, fears, and needs? How does a writer speak to those issues, understanding and caring about the daily lives of those who make up this audience? How can your story speak to its intended audience, entertaining and, perhaps, even transforming them in the process?

What do you expect an audience to feel at certain places in your script? When do you expect them to laugh? If you don't know, they won't know. When do you expect them to fall in love with your character? If you're not sure, they won't be sure. When do you want them to cry? When do you want them to be concerned? When will their hands start to sweat out of worry and fright? When will they grab the hand of the person next to them for reassurance? You can't force these things to happen. You have to know an audience well enough to understand what they respond to, and then make sure that these elements are authentically rendered in your script. This doesn't mean manipulating the audience, or adding on and sticking in moments that can make the audience feel used. There's an honest cry and a dishonest cry. The honest cry enhances an audience's experience and makes its members realize how much they care about these characters on the screen. It's cathartic. It may even lead to personal transformations of individual audience members. The dishonest cry cheapens an audience experience and makes its members realize, in retrospect, that a writer didn't care about them, so they feel angry and used.

When everything in a script works well, its characters and the emotions they generate in the audience are authentic and organic. Learning to understand an audience and speak to it is part of becoming a masterful screenwriter. This requires honing your work to find the best ways to authentically portray your characters' responses so that the audience will feel along with your characters. This isn't manipulation, this is art.

How do you help your characters speak to an audience? How do you use the techniques you've read in this book to keep your audience connected from beginning to end and to give them something to take with them as they leave the theater?

EDUCATING THE AUDIENCE

Does the audience need to be educated about some aspect of your story before they can understand it? Most films contain some element or aspect that the audience doesn't know about but needs to know in order to understand your story and connect with its characters. In *The Color of Money*, the game of pool was explained in the first few minutes of the film. After that, we knew what we had to know and could follow the game, knowing what and which characters to root for.

In *Titanic*, the "unsinkable" design of the ship was clarified for the audience. With that knowledge we could see through the point of view of the characters, and thrill to their journey.

In *Elizabeth* and *Shakespeare in Love*, we had to have some education about the context of the times. Once we knew that, we understood the limited roles open to Viola as a woman within Elizabethan society, and we understood the creative and business pressures on Shakespeare. Once we understood the context, we knew who and what to root for.

In *L.A. Confidential*, we needed to know something about L.A. in the 1940s and 1950s. Through voice-overs and visuals, we were taken back to that time. Once we understood that world, we could understand the story's intricacies and the corruption. In *Jerry Maguire* and *Rain Man,* we had to understand two very specific financial worlds: one of sports agents and one of the gray market for cars. In *Absence of Malice* and *Broadcast News*, we had to understand the world of journalism. In *Remains of the Day* and *Howard's End* we had to understand the English class structure.

To give the audience what they need to know, a writer's research has to be accurate. When a writer's research is accurate, every detail matches up with whatever we already know about the subject. The onscreen world created from this research seems real because every fact is credible. When a writer is not accurate, the audience feels it. Inaccuracies throw audience members out of the story, since at least some people in the audience will recognize a writer's lack of research. As a result, these audience members will be distanced from a film. Once an audience has been distanced because something in a film is incredible, rarely will they totally reconnect with that film. In fact, most of the time the audience will distrust everything that follows. Just like it's difficult in a relationship to recover from a lie or a betrayal, an audience has trouble responding to the story when it no longer trusts a writer.

Accurate research can keep audiences connected to a film, even when its story wouldn't ordinarily be of interest to them. Great research shows that a writer has been there, knows that world, and is placing characters solidly in their proper context.

I have little interest in pool or baseball or basketball, but I am pulled in by the richly detailed contexts of *The Color of Money*, *Field of Dreams*, and *Hoosiers*. I know little about the world of cotton mills, but *Norma Rae* fascinates me. It pulls me into her issues and concerns, not just because the film's themes are universal, but because of the film's seeming accuracy and unexpected and interesting details. I believed the world of *Out of Africa* with its coffee plantations and various tribes and types of railroad cars. If I believe in these detailed worlds, I can then believe in the emotions, issues, goals, dreams, and yearnings of their characters.

This, of course, doesn't preclude a writer's imagination. A writer starts with an accurately depicted world and then moves beyond it to create a new and different world. We know about fortune-tellers, but in *Big*, we learn about a fortune-teller who can make a boy into a man. We know about fast cars, but in *Back to the Future* we see a car that can go so fast that it takes a boy into the past. We know that sometimes girls do dress as boys, and in *Shakespeare in Love*, we see a girl act the part of a boy and get away with it. These are not results of a writer's inaccurate research, but of originality that still rings true enough to help us suspend our disbelief, because it all makes sense. Rather than being jarred out of our real world, we are enticed, captured, and pulled into a detailed screen world.

FOCUSING THE AUDIENCE

As screenwriters gain skill, they begin to learn the intricacies of the audience and develop a sense of how it will, could, or might respond to certain aspects of their scripts.

How will the audience know that a film is a comedy? How and when can a writer set up the comedy so that the audience is aware of the genre and is captured immediately? A writer needs to know where the laughs are, and needs to offer some within the first few minutes of a film. Some writers, such as the Zucker brothers (the *Airplane!* spoofs and *the Naked Gun* series), make sure that every script page contains several laughs. Other writers might want to write films that just make audiences smile. The laughs in *When Harry Met Sally* are not as broad as in the Zuckers' spoofs, and they are not meant to be. You can feel Nora Ephron's skill because she knew her characters so well that we could move with them emotionally and, at the same time, be amused by them.

If a film's style is meant to be outrageous, how will the writer and the director prepare the audience for it? How did they prepare the audience for *There's Something About Mary*? Or for the outrageous behavior in *Liar Liar*? Or for the drama mixed with comedy in *Terms of Endearment*? A writer makes sure that a film's style is set up within the first few pages, and then remains consistent throughout.

I often tell clients to choose the scene that best expresses the style they are striving for, and then make that scene the model for all scenes throughout the entire script. I recommend that clients set up their style immediately—certainly within the first minute or two of the film—so that the audience gets it. Then, I have them wash the entire script in this style. That doesn't mean that every scene in an outrageous movie has to be outrageous. Once an outrageous style has been well set up, it's possible to move into more tender moments, as we find in both *There's Something About Mary* and *Liar Liar*. Once the audience understands a film's style, a writer can play with it and expand on it.

Sometimes writers find a script's style as they write. It's not unusual to discover the style they wish to use fifty or eighty pages into the script. In these cases, I recommend that they go back throughout the entire script and do a rewrite, so that all scenes are consistent with this style.

Regardless of the style chosen, writers should have some sense of how they *want* the audience to respond and how the audience *will* respond.

If a film is a love story, a writer should know where the audience will fall in love with the characters, and when they'll be convinced that these two people belong together. If a film is a three-hanky tear-jerker, a writer should know where the audience will start crying, and how long it'll cry. This sort of film might require adding a few pages to its resolution, so the audience has a chance to get itself together before the lights go on at the end. This type of film also might require knowing where to add some comic relief.

TRANSFORMING THE AUDIENCE

In the best of all worlds, what would be a writer's fondest hope? Many writers I've talked to have a secret, hardly-told-it-to-anyone, deep-down hope to transform their audiences. They want their films to mean something, to make a difference, to cause audience members to make a new decision, to find greater happiness, to overcome resistance, to take social action, to love more and respond more.

Some writers think they can best transform an audience by telling them what to do. Sometimes this includes preaching, giving advice, or using one character as the writer's mouthpiece. The mouthpiece invariably gives long-winded intellectual speeches that rarely convert anyone but merely preachy to the already-converted. This form of persuasion rarely works.

We have probably all experienced transformational films that called us to some new action that, on some level, changed our lives. You might have become more involved in social action and social justice as a result of seeing *Norma Rae* or *Powwow Highway* or *Schindler's List* or *The Milagro Beanfield War*. You might have let down your resistance and found that the love of your life was also the friend of your life as a result of seeing *When Harry Met Sally* or *Tootsie*. You might have worked harder at some physical ability as a result of seeing *Rocky* or found greater artistic commitment as a result of seeing *Shine* or *The Piano*. Maybe you got more in touch with your inner child as a result of seeing *The Kid*.

To transform audience members, a film need not be deep and profound, but it should be an honest depiction of some part of the human condition. A film that probably had the greatest effect on my personal life was, of all things, *City Slickers*. You may laugh at this choice, but any good film can have the potential to transform us.

In 1988, I saw an ad for a cattle drive. It never occurred to me that the ordinary person could actually move cattle from one place to another. The ad reawakened my childhood love of horseback riding and of the Western, but I never acted upon it until I saw *City Slickers*. The film motivated me not to wait any longer. A year after the movie came out, I helped move 600 head of cattle across the Montana-Wyoming border. Interestingly, ranches had record numbers of city folk sign up for cattle drives right after *City Slickers* was released.

For many of us city folk, seeing *City Slickers* was the impetus to do something that looked like fun. But for me, it was transforming. It reawakened my love of the outdoors. It made me realize that there was a cowgirl inside me that I admired and respected. It inspired me to put a lingering idea into motion. Since my initial cattle drive, I've taken at least one riding vacation each year, and I even won a blue ribbon at a Denver horse show. Horseback riding has motivated me to lose weight and exercise. It has put balance into my life. In April, 2003, I bought my first horse. All of this can be traced back to the catalyst of this film.

Think of films that have had a transforming effect on your life. How did they chnage you? How much did they change you?

In most cases, audience transformation begins with the transformation of a character on screen. Writer Akiva Goldsman and director Ron Howard told me that audience members reported greater compassion and understanding of mental illness as a result of seeing *A Beautiful Mind*. Writer Tom Schulman and actor Robin Williams told me about people changing jobs as a result of seeing *Dead Poets Society*. When an audience identifies with an onscreen character who is transformed, the issue that drove that character's transformation is shared by many in the audience. Undoubtedly many pending decisions sit inside the heads of audience members as they watch a film. If they see a character make the right decision, it inspires them to make a right choice, consciously or unconsciously. Movies can be a kind of sounding board for our own struggles and issues.

Sometimes, audience members transform their lives because of watching what happens to a character who doesn't transform. I find no transformations in *Goodfellas*, but I can imagine someone in the audience transforming because of watching the many negative effects of certain life choices.

Most stories that transform audiences start with an audience-identification character. This is usually the protagonist. We move into this character's world and believe in it, at least for the course of a film. It's important that this character be similar to us in some way. Otherwise we'll have difficulty vicariously taking this character's journey and, at the end of the film, using it to motivate our own lives.

We can connect with this character if you, a writer, use all the dramatic elements at your disposal to help us connect: through the thematic journey, by exploring character conflicts and relationships and context, by making sure your protagonist is the same general age as the core audience, and by dealing with the issues that the character and the audience would be dealing with at that age.

You can broaden the possibilities that your script will generate audience transformations by creating a multi-dimensional world. This can include characters of different ages with different but related issues. *On Golden Pond* created three generations with three different issues. No matter what age you were, one of these characters probably had an issue similar to yours.

In addition to creating characters of different ages, create characters of different racial backgrounds. Many people think we live in a world that's all one color, but it isn't. Films are losing millions of potential viewers by ignoring the diversity of people who make up their audiences. This means that a writer has to open up and even research other cultures and other races in order to write about them and understand their issues and to broaden the world depicted in film.

And don't forget the women. We make up more than 50% of the population, but to look at most films, one would think that we are all but invisible. Sometimes I wonder what kind of world most writers live in. It often seems they've never met women who are powerful, assertive, courageous, strong, and multi-dimensional. Real-life women tend to be far more exciting than we've yet seen in film. Studios could be losing millions of dollars through ignorance and through the sometimes subtle, sometimes overt, racism, ageism, and sexism of the film industry.

WHAT TO DO ABOUT IT?

Writers have a tendency to blame others for the ageism, racism, and sexism that we see on screen. Some think it's the fault of the studios and the producers. Others think it's the audience's fault. To a great extent, all of this is true. But if change doesn't begin with you, the writer, where will it start?

Some writers confront these issues by making sure that their films have a broad range of characters. They find that if they simply write "a black lawyer" or a "hispanic judge," the casting agent will follow these character descriptions. By creating a socially broader world through supporting roles, you also create the possibility of speaking to more people in the audience and, therefore, creating films that make a difference.

But you can go further. The critical and commercial success of such films as *Do the Right Thing*, *Boyz N the Hood*, *Crouching Tiger, Hidden Dragon*, *Born on the Fourth of July*, *Shine*, *Waiting to Exhale*, *The First Wives Club*, *A Beautiful Mind*, and *Rain Man* attests to the potential success of films with both major and supporting characters who are non-white, of different ages, of different genders, and some of whom are disabled. The myth that only white men can successfully carry a film is a falsehood that needs to be changed in the minds of writers and producers in order to create a new generation of great films that speak to large audiences.

IN THE REALM OF THE SENSES

You can also broaden your film's audience appeal by writing with all of your senses. Think of the visual aspects of your scenes. Think about sounds. Think about touch. Some films have shown a sense of taste: Think of the delectable meals from *Remains of the Day* and *The Age of Innocence* and *Chocolate*. Occasionally a film shows the sense of smell: You might remember the moment in *Dead Poets Society* when Neil's father smelled gun powder, before seeing the gun and his dead son.

If you make sure that all five senses are explored in your film, you have the potential to engage your audience on many levels and, therefore, help them identify with your characters. Although some of these sensory moments will be added by the director and the actors, it's still a writer's responsibility to show the moments in the script where characters notice and observe and respond to visual, auditory, and kinesthetic stimuli.

Bring in the visuals. Think about the flying scene in *Out of Africa* and the barnraising scene in *Witness* and the overall visual celebration of *Moulin Rouge!*

Remember the sound. You might remember the powerful sound of gunfire in *Platoon* and *Born on the Fourth of July*. The barking dogs in *101 Dalmatians*. The sound of the laser swords in *Star Wars* and of the tractor in *A Simple Story*. The sound of the ball hitting the glove in *Bull Durham* and *The Rookie* and *A League of Their Own*.

Film can hint at the sense of touch so that we feel certain moments in our bodies. Perhaps you can feel the soap in *As Good As It Gets*, as Melvin washes his hands again and again, or the rose petals in the bathtub in *American Beauty*.

As you add sensory material to your script, also add emotions. Show people *experiencing* touch. Show their hearts responding, not just their heads. We transform through being hit in the heart or the gut. When your characters feel, we feel.

CONNECTING WITH THE AUDIENCE

Transformation is ultimately about choice. Do we want to change or not? And if so, how do we do it? Author Thom Hartmann said in a speech at the Palm Springs Story Conference in 2002 that "people change not by taking something away from them, but by giving them an additional tool. Since the self is a collection of all that we are, people resist if something is being taken away. For instance, if someone fights at every opportunity, for them to give up fighting means to give up part of themselves. But if the person is told that fighting, in certain circumstances, can be a good thing, they might be more receptive to picking up the additional skill of negotiation."

Hartmann also discussed how change can happen by giving variety to a film's protagonist's point of view. When watching a film, we are usually inside the eyes of the main character, looking out at the world. We see what that character sees, thereby enhancing our identification with the protagonist. This subjective point of view helps us identify with the protagonist. We might begin to feel that if s/he can change, then maybe we too can change, since we're so much like each other.

Film also contains an omniscient, objective point of view, which is our sense of ourselves as we watch the protagonist. To do this, we move from the subjective point of view of behavior to the objective point of view. We distance ourselves as we watch the protagonist's behavior. This helps us put both the character and ourselves in perspective. As a result, we observe the consequences of onscreen behavior. We observe how a character got from the beginning to the end of a film and what tools were needed to achieve the character's desired goal. We can then decide if the result the protagonist achieves is the result we want to achieve in our lives. Therefore, audience transformation comes about through the combination of direct emotional involvement with a film as it's being watched and, later, by objectifying the story, remembering scenes, reflecting on character actions, and seeing a character's arc as being like our own arc.

Transformation is about possibilities. You can't force a change in other people. But you can present a potential new behavior that they may not have thought about or may not have thought was possible to accomplish.

Audience members transform when they are given choices, showing the consequences of those choices, and giving your characters and the audience new tools that make it possible to create change. You model new behavior through your characters, and the audience members can, through them, acquire the know-how to make a change, if they so desire.

Learning to transform the audience requires writers to tune in to what they know about individual and group responses to various stimuli and to develop a sense of communication, identification, and empathy with their chosen audience. If a writer doesn't have some sense of where the audience is emotionally, transforming them will be difficult.

MAKING SURE THE AUDIENCE GETS IT

How do we know that the audience will get it? For an audience to get a film, writers must be in tune with their stories' emotions. If a writer doesn't feel, the characters won't feel. If the characters don't feel, the audience won't feel.

A writer needs to make sure that the script is clear: the story is clear, the characters are clear, the theme is clear. Some writers seem to want to confuse the audience. Mystery is fine. Confusion isn't.

To feel in touch with an audience, writers often have others read their work and give them feedback. Naturally, I'm a firm believer in feedback, given that I've been a script consultant for more than twenty years. I also have readers and consultants for all my books. I wouldn't dream of handing in a book to a publisher without having seven to ten readers give me notes. I choose my readers carefully, so that they represent my reading audience. In the case of this book, many of my readers were experienced screenwriters who have had their scripts optioned, sold, and sometimes made into films. I often hire a literary consultant to go over my work after the readers have given me feedback. Then I take my editor's suggestions seriously, since s/he's my last objective responder before the book is published. Each of these readers represents a part of the book's audience. They let me know when there's a problem and offer me possible solutions.

I recommend that screenwriters get intelligent feedback before trying to sell a script. This feedback might come from fellow screenwriters or from a class or friends or a story analyst and/or a script consultant. Sometimes a writer or producer will have a read-through of a script to hear the words acted. When a script is sold, various development people—including analysts and the director and actors—will all give feedback.

Many writers don't want feedback because they've experienced subjective, negative critiques that were misleading. Don't ask negative people to read your work. You don't need them.

Choose your readers carefully, and if someone isn't serving your intent and the intent of the script, find someone else. There's no reason to have bad feedback when there are plenty of people who can give you constructive critiques. Ultimately, your readers are part of your audience, so if they're not touched, your audience won't be.

STORIES CAN MAKE A DIFFERENCE

Stories are powerful. They can change your life as you figure out which ones you want to tell and how you want to tell them. Stories can change individual audience members, presenting them with insights and possibilities and models of alternative behaviors. Stories can change our culture. They can serve as a model of good. They can give possibilities. They can encourage. Stories can be so toxic that they pull down civilizations or so potent that they build them up.

There is nothing that a story can't be and nothing that a story has to be. Storytelling is an art that is complex enough that thousands of books have not yet explored all its dimensions. Stories are deep enough that we don't yet know all the ways they can change our psyches. As one of the most sensory—and thereby powerful—mediums, film helps us identify with a story and characters who help connect us with all of humanity, letting us know that film stories are our stories. When done well, the art of screenwriting has the potential to transport us to new worlds and transform our lives.